# With Liberty
# &
# Justice For All

*Christian Politics Made Simple*

Joseph Morecraft, III

Introduction by Dr. Rousas John Rushdoony

Scripture references quoted from
the *Holy Bible: King James Version* and the
*Holy Bible: New American Standard Version*


Cover Design by
Merriana Branan of Art & Design, Atlanta, GA


Published by

# Onward
# Press

P. O. Box 4690
Sevierville, TN 37864

Printed in the United States of America
ISBN 0-925591-15-7

## *For The Glory Of God*

*Now therefore, O kings, show discernment; take warning, O judges of the earth. Serve the Lord with reverence, and rejoice with trembling. Kiss the Son, lest He become angry, and you perish in the way, for His wrath may soon be kindled. How blessed are all who take refuge in Him.*

— Psalm 2:10-12

*Dedicated to*

*My Loving Wife, Becky*

# Table of Contents

INTRODUCTION

# The Theology of Politics

by Dr. Rousas John Rushdoony

An area of study much neglected in the past two centuries or more is *the theology of politics.* Political thinking has become secularized and humanistic to the point that to speak about the relationship of God to politics is for many to introduce an alien factor into the discussion. For too many churchmen, the extent of political concern by the Church should be limited to praying for those in authority. This is a beggarly reduction of the meaning of the faith.

The starting point of biblical thought is the fact of creation. *In the beginning God created the heaven and the earth* (Genesis 1:1). This creating God is not some vaguely non-partisan deity who belongs equally to a variety of religions and philosophies. He is the triune God; He is the Father of Jesus Christ. God the Son, in His eternal being, is He by whom all things were created. John begins his gospel by making this identification:

1. *In the beginning was the Word, and the Word was with God, and the Word was God.*

2. *The same was in the beginning with God.*

3. *All things were made by him; and without him was not any thing made that was made* (John 1:1-3).

Thus politics cannot be a neutral realm. In a universe which is totally God's creation, there can be no neutral realm, no, not a neutral thought nor atom. All things are under God and His government.

Moreover, we are plainly told that He *who is the blessed and only Potentate, the King of kings, and*

*Lord of lords* (II Timothy 6:15) is our Lord Jesus Christ. This means that, *first,* there can be no religiously neutral political system. All are either under Christ or against Him. There can be religious freedom, but not neutrality. To imagine that God left some areas of His creation outside His purpose and government has no foundation in Scripture.

*Second,* this means that we must have a theology of politics, one based on the whole word of God. Such a theology must apply Scripture to every facet of political life. It must stress the duty to God of all who hold office. The U. S. Constitution provides an *oath* of office; the framers saw oaths as a biblical fact; an oath places the office, the office-holders, and the social order *under God.*

*Third,* because social order is a moral fact, and morality is a branch of theology, a lack of faith among the people, and an indifference to theological order by the state, soon means a moral decay and then social collapse.

*Fourth,* a civil government is not a church and is thus not involved in church matters nor in ecclesiastical doctrines, but it must affirm a biblical faith if it is to avoid social collapse. Politics divorced from God and His Word cannot provide a valid moral order. Instead, it becomes a corrosive force for decadence. This does not mean a creedal stand by the state. After all, more than a few churches profess great creeds and believe none of them. A sound theology of politics must begin in the lives of the people and manifest itself in the churches. If it is not in the people nor in the Church, it will not be in the state.

*Fifth,* in terms of Scripture, Church and state are both ministries under God. The Church is *a* ministry of grace, and the state is *a* ministry of justice. Note that in neither case should we limit the ministries. While the church is the main means of the ministry of grace, we dare not forget that God's grace reaches men through a variety of channels. The same is true of civil government; the world would be a bleak and fearful place if justice existed only within the machinery of the state. Our parents routinely administered justice to us, as do churches, employers, and a variety of groups and persons. To be effective, grace and justice must be present in every sphere of life. We must not restrict God's work to official channels! To do so is to limit God, a dangerous thing to attempt. We must see the ministerial nature of civil government without limiting justice to the state.

In the 1600s, Richard Steele wrote on *The Religious Tradesman,* an application of Scripture to the world of business. He began by declaring that religion, meaning Christianity, is "the great business of life." Any theory of politics which neglects biblical faith as its premise will result in quackery and will be productive of social disorder.

Joe Morecraft, III has written a study of political theology. He tells us that liberty and justice have as their necessary premise Christianity, and without that faith society ends in slavery and injustice. He writes with ability, intelligence, and forthrightness. His is not a closet faith nor is he a trumpet sounding retreat. Rather, with faith in the triune and sovereign God, he is a warrior for the truth.

# CHAPTER ONE

# *The Origin Of Civil Government*

## Politics and Christian Faith

Let every person be in subjection to the governing authorities. For there is no authority except from God, and those which exist are established by God.

Therefore he who resists authority has opposed the ordinance of God; and they who have opposed will receive condemnation upon themselves. For rulers are not a cause of fear for good behavior, but for evil.

Do you want to have no fear of authority? Do what is good, and you will have praise from the same; for it is a minister of God to you for good. But if you do what is evil, be afraid; for it does not bear the sword for nothing; for it is a minister of God, an avenger who brings wrath upon the one who practices evil.

Wherefore it is necessary to be in subjection, not only because of wrath, but also for conscience sake. For because of this you also pay taxes, for rulers are servants of God, devoting themselves to this very thing. Render to all what is due them: tax to whom tax is due; custom to whom custom; fear to whom fear; honor to whom honor (Romans 13:1-7 NASV).

Here is the biblical basis for a Christian view of politics. Allow it to shape all your views on candidates, legislation, public policy and the whole range of critical issues facing us today.

We can clearly understand Romans 13:1-7 only as we read it in the light of Romans 12:1-2 and in context with the whole of chapters 12 and 13.

I urge you therefore, brethren, by the mercies of God, to present your bodies a living and holy sacrifice, acceptable to God, which is your spiritual service of worship. And do not be conformed to this world, but be transformed by the renewing of your mind, that you

> may prove what the will of God is, that which is good
> and acceptable and perfect (Romans 12:1-2 NASV).

When we become aware of the fact that we are recipients of God's saving mercy in Christ, it will have a dramatic impact on the entirety of our lives. We will unconditionally surrender our lives and thoughts to the service of Jesus Christ, becoming more and more renewed and governed by His revealed Word. That is the point of Romans 12:1-2.

Romans 12 and 13 bring out the fact that this undivided devotion to Jesus Christ will control the entirety of our lives, inside and out. It will govern our relationships with other Christians in the Church (12:3-16) and with non-Christians in the world (12:17-21). Furthermore, it will manifest itself in our political views (13:1-7) and in our dealings with people in general (13:8-10).

If we believe that God's mercy makes a total claim on us, and that our devotion to the rule of Christ must be unlimited, it will make a difference in the way we look at the authority and demands of the civil government, and in the nature and extent of our allegiance to the civil government.

Whole-hearted involvement in politics and careful, correct thinking about political issues are not distractions or options for the Christian. The whole of the Christian life is to be dedicated to the Lord. It all must be governed by His Word. Every facet of human existence must be dedicated to Him who is *the Ruler of the kings of the earth* (Revelation 1:5).

To be careless or haphazard in political concerns

is to be careless and haphazard in our obedience to Christ, and to be ungrateful for His redeeming mercy, which, having bought us, demands all we have, all we are and all we do — *you are not your own. ... For you have been bought with a price: therefore glorify God in your body* (I Corinthians 6:19-20).

Romans 13:1-7 sets forth two duties: (1) the duty of citizens to the civil government and (2) the duty of the civil government toward God. Since the civil government has been instituted and authorized by God for the maintenance of His moral order and for the punishment of criminals who violate that order, the civil government is duty-bound to submit to God, just as the citizen is duty-bound to submit to the civil government. This is not to say that the civil government may never be criticized regardless of what it does. Nor does it mean that it must be obeyed no matter what it demands.

Our highest allegiance must always be to God in Christ. Loyalty to Him supercedes and determines all other loyalties. Therefore, if the demands of the state (civil government) come in conflict with the demands of God, the Christian's allegiance to God must take precedence over his allegiance to the state. When Peter and John were forbidden by the municipal authorities to preach the gospel, they, nevertheless, continued to preach the gospel, replying: *We must obey God rather than men* (Acts 5:29). (See also Acts 4:19f; Exodus 1:17, 20; Daniel 3:16f.)

The Church and individual Christians have a prophetic responsibility toward the civil government. As Isaiah, Jeremiah, Daniel, and Elijah did, we are to call the civil government to repentance when it passes legislation and institutes policies which are contrary to the law of God.

Elijah confronted King Ahab because he had *forsaken the commandments of the Lord* (I Kings 18:18). We find God's servants addressing the political powers in this same prophetic manner and correcting them for their departures from God's law. The most familiar instance of this is John the Baptist rebuking Herod for his adultery, and then losing his head for it. Martin Luther said the Church is called upon to "lick the fur" of the state, i.e., to keep it clean.

Because the state is said to be a "minister of God," does not mean that it must always be obeyed regardless of what it does. To say that the state is a "minister of God" is not to say that it is necessarily that at all points.

Through sin it can become the opposite of what it was meant to be, just as ministers in the Church, by teaching heresy, can become "angels of light," who are to be opposed, avoided and expelled from the Church. In the book of Revelation, an anti-Christian state, like Rome under Nero in his later years, is called a "beast," Revelation 13, because it is a threat to liberty, justice, and the Church of Christ.

There is nothing in Romans 13:1-7 which is not taught in the Old Testament. Paul's Holy Spirit-inspired doctrine of civil government is firmly rooted in the perspective of the Holy Spirit-inspired Old Testament. In his book, *Theonomy and Christian Ethics,* Greg Bahnsen has pointed out the political parallels of the Old Testament and the New Testament (Presbyterian and Reformed Publishing Company, Phillipsburg, N.J. pp. 317-401):

> (1) God sovereignly appoints and removes political rulers. (2) Political rulers are not to be resisted. (3) They bear religious titles. (4) They act for God in the execution of capital criminals. (5) They are to deter evil and honor good. (6) They must rule in accordance with God's law. (7) They are subject to criticism whenever they disobey God's law.

These parallels between Romans and the Old Testament prove that the Bible is unified in its teaching of the nature and role of civil government. The Old and New Testaments are not at odds with each other on this subject. The New builds upon the Old. Therefore this subject of politics is a highly spiritual one, because a "spiritual" subject is a "Spirit-produced" subject, i.e., a truth taken from the Spirit-produced Word of God (I Corinthians 2:13).

## The Supremacy Of God

Romans 13:1-2 present us with the basic premise of Christian politics: *There is no power but from God. The powers that be are ordained by God.* "Powers" refers to civil authorities with the God-given right and power to rule in the jurisdiction of civil issues assigned to it by God Himself in the Bible.

The empasis here is on *the Supremacy of God*, not the supremacy of the state. The point is *not* that because all civil institutions are established by God, therefore, they are supreme and beyond criticism. Rather, the point is that because all civil institutions are ordained by God, therefore *God* is supreme over them all and He is beyond criticism.

God is supreme over all individuals and institutions (Jeremiah 10:6f). He is the source of all civil authority. And His government over men and nations is universal, unlimited and unrestricted. More specifically, Jesus Christ is *the King of kings, and Lord of lords* (Revelation 19:16). All authority in heaven and on earth has been given to Him (Matthew 28:18). He is *the ruler of the kings of the earth* (Revelation 1:5).

There is a diversity of human governments: self-government, family government, Church government, and civil government. Each sphere has its clearly defined functions, limitations and powers. One institution may not usurp the rights and powers of another with impunity. All are accountable to God who is their Supreme Origin. His governing rule is over them all (Isaiah 9:6). Therefore, all are equally accountable to Him. The Church is institutionally and functionally separate from the state, but the Church is no more accountable to God than the state, for both are equally and totally accountable to God.

Both citizens and state are subject to God's authority. Both are under obligation to their Lord and to His revealed will. Citizens are to submit to political authority because it originates with God. Political institutions are to submit to the revealed will of God, because He is their Origin, Proprietor and Lord.

All forms of human governments draw their authority, power and jurisdiction from God, not from the will of the people nor the consent of the governed, because governments do not originate with the people, but with God. The voice of the people is NOT the voice of God. The voice of God is His revealed will, which is the Holy Bible (II Timothy 3:16). Therefore, civil, political and judicial authorities are to obey God alone, regardless of the will and preferences of the people. God calls upon all elected and appointed officials to study His law

> all the days of his life, that He may learn to fear the Lord his God, by carefully observing all the words of this law and these statutes, that his heart may not be lifted up above his countrymen and that he may not turn aside from the commandment, to the right or the left (Deuteronomy 17:19f).

The U. S. Constitution reflects this basic premise in its establishment of a republic under God rather than a democracy. The two are not synonymous. A democracy is a nation governed by the majority; and a republic is a nation governed by law. A Christian Republic is a nation governed by a constitution which is rooted in biblical law, administered by representatives of the constitution democratically elected by the citizens.

In a democracy the whims and fancies of the

majority, manipulated by the media or elitist power-brokers, become the law of the land. In such a situation neither our lives nor our private possessions are safe. In a democracy if the majority of people believe abortion-on-demand is permissible, the lives of all unborn citizens are jeopardized. If the majority of people want to use political force to redistribute the wealth from producers and savers to bureaucrats, no one's property is safe. If the majority believe that everyone over sixty-five years of age should be required to commit suicide so as not to be a drain on society's resources, no elderly person is safe.

But, in a Christian Republic, governed by constitutional law rooted in biblical law, all life and property is safe. If the majority demand abortion or the redistribution of the wealth or the death of the elderly, none of these things will take place, because, in a republic, law rules, not the majority.

A constitution based on the Bible would protect the sanctity of human life and the legitimacy of the private ownership of property. Moreover, if the majority want lax divorce laws and the legalization of pornography, such immorality is not allowed because of the constitutional protection of the family.

If the majority want the education of children to be controlled by the state rather than the family, such an assault on parental authority will not take place, again, because of the protection of the God-given powers of the family.

If the majority want the weekly Sabbath to be infringed upon by industry and legislation, nevertheless, the Sabbath will be preserved, because of the constitutional protection of the Christian Sabbath. (People living in a Christian Republic experience true freedom while those under the "mob rule" of democracies become slaves because democracies soon degenerate into socialist states and dictatorships.)

Because political authority and power come from God, all political institutions must submit to His rule and recognize their total accountability to His total sovereignty and to His written demands of that sovereignty in the Bible. If they choose not to do so, they must be prepared to suffer under His judgment, because of their rebellion against His government. No state can take a neutral stance towards the God of the Bible and survive (Psalm 2). All states must "kiss the Son" or perish!

This emphasis on the political supremacy of God over the state is what distinguishes humanist politics from Christian politics. Christianity believes that, in political issues, God and His written will are supreme. Humanism believes that in politics man and his will are supreme. Thus, humanism is a futile attempt on the part of unregenerate man to banish God from human society.

Humanistic (anti-Christian) politics takes two basic forms: collectivism and libertarianism. Collectivism emphasizes the "group" (state) over the individual members of the group. It believes that political authority is drawn from the state and that human liberties are granted by the state to the individual. These liberties may be taken away by the state who gave them, if it is for the good of the group. Might makes right in a godless social order. In the Soviet Union, the supreme example of collectivism, millions of individuals have been slaughtered for the "good of the state."

Libertarianism emphasizes the individual over the group. It believes that political authority is drawn from the individual, not the group. Nothing must be allowed to restrict individual freedom, not even a system of ethical absolutes from God. Therefore, according to libertarianism, it is wrong to outlaw abortion or homosexuality, because to do so would infringe on individual freedom.

Collectivism believes in the supreme sovereignty of the state. Libertarianism believes in the supreme sovereignty of the individual. And non-Christian forms of capitalism believe in the supreme sovereignty of the market. But Christianity believes in the supreme sovereignty of the triune God alone, before Whom both the individual and the group are obligated and privileged to bow.

Both libertarianism and collectivism are idolatrous, enslaving, dehumanizing, murderous and suicidal. Collectivism/communism is responsible for the deaths of 200 million people since the Bolshevik Revolution under Lenin. Libertarianism in the United States has resulted in the legal murder of nearly 20 million people through abortion. Human-

ism is deadly! *Those who hate God love death* says
Proverbs 8:36.

The supremacy of God in all political matters has
implications for the citizen's responsibility toward
the state, and the state's responsibility toward God.
The citizen, Christian and non-Christian, must be
in subjection to the civil government and must
respect it, remembering that he is submitting to it
for the sake of Christ and that his loyalty to Christ
supercedes his loyalty to the state.

We gladly recognize the jurisdiction and authority of the civil magistrate and willingly and actively
pledge our allegiance to that authority under God.
Furthermore, we recognize that to resist civil authorities lawlessly and unbiblically is in actuality
resisting the ordinance of God, which will bring His
judgment upon us. On the other hand, the civil
government must be in subjection to God and to His
law-order. It must subject itself to His supremacy,
obey and enforce His law within a nation.

As individual citizens, we must be sure we clearly
understand what this means for us: *He who resists
authority has opposed the ordinance of God.* He who
does so puts himself in rebellion against God's order
for life and society. If God is supreme over all, then
every individual citizen must be in respectful submission to the civil government.

Some, who consider themselves conservative,
patriotic citizens have a flippant and contemptuous
attitude toward civil government. But the Bible
tells us that that is an improper and dangerous

attitude for a Christian. Since political powers are established by God, we must gladly submit to their authority. The word subjection in verses 2 and 5 is more inclusive than the word obedience. In other words Christians not only have the duty to obey civil authorities, we also are to recognize their authority over us and actively and gladly participate in the duty of submitting to them.

What are the powers that be in the United States? Some try to evade the force of our text by saying that those powers are, exclusively, the U. S. Constitution. But it is obvious from Romans 13:1-7 that those powers must also include those civil magistrates who administer that Constitution, i.e., those who have been elected to rule over us in places of civil authority.

Notice what happens to us if we do not submit to the political ordinance of God: *They who resist authority ... will receive condemnation upon themselves.* It is a serious thing not to submit to the civil government. If we do not do so, God views our actions and attitudes as resistance to His moral and political order. Such refusal to honor the civil government brings "condemnation" or divine judgment upon us.

Conservatives and liberals who act flippantly and contemptuously toward the civil government are earning for themselves the terrifying judgment of Almighty God. Some "conservatives" have a hostile attitude to civil government because they hold the idea that the civil government is a lesser evil to anarchy, something they must tolerate to have social harmony.

As long as they have this idea, they will have a less than adequate understanding of what their responsibility to the civil government should be. The ordinance of civil government is not a lesser evil. It is ordained by God. It is a gift which God has given to assist in the maintenance of His moral order on earth so that people can live out their lives in freedom and dignity, carrying out their vocations under God's blessing without disturbance. Submission to civil authorities means receiving them as gifts from God for our benefit.

After God purged the earth with a flood, He turned this new world over to Noah and made a covenant with him in which He said in effect: "Noah, I want you to conquer this new earth, and I am going to give you some institutions to help you do it. Maintain these institutions and you will succeed. I will see to it" (Genesis 8-9).

Those embryonic institutions God gave Noah for the preservation of human society are the family, the civil government and the dominion mandate (or work ethic). As long as Noah and his family respected these institutions, this new world order, which began with the subsiding of the flood, would continue in place as the kingdom of Christ progressed in the conquest of all opposing kingdoms.

So, the civil government is not a lesser evil we must tolerate. It is a gracious gift of our God to His people so that we can be protected from the lawless in order to live out our lives in peace (I Timothy 2:1). When we understand this truth, it will motivate us to be more consistent in our respectful submission to political institutions.

We are living during the most critical decade in the history of our republic. Unless Christians can come to power in the United States within the next few years, in order to give the Church room and time to proclaim the gospel of Christ freely, we are going to see many years of devastation in our beloved land.

These are solemn times for our nation, but this does not imply that we are to act out of panic and desperation as revolutionaries. The hold anti-Christianity has on our nation must be broken, but not by any method. Only the faithful application of the Bible to our problems and strategies will work, and only then as a gracious God chooses to bless our efforts. We must make sure we have a biblical basis for everything we do to save America or we will get nowhere.

So, we must not act and think like revolutionaries who use violence to accomplish their ends. We must be true reformers who take the Word of God and work intensely, vigorously, and perseveringly toward the Christian Reconstruction of our apostate culture, beginning with the capture of the hearts and minds of men and women with the gospel.

The second great implication of the supremacy of God over politics applies to the duty of the political institution, as well as to the duty of the individual citizen. The individual's duty is clear: he must submit to the powers that be. The state's duty is equally clear: it must submit to Almighty God. If God is supreme, the state must bow to the supremacy of God over it.

Jesus teaches us that we are to render to Caesar (i.e., the civil government), the things that belong to him (Matthew 22:21). To understand this statement, we must notice the context in which it was spoken. Jesus and His followers were looking at a Roman coin. They were concerned about paying taxes. Jesus asked them, *Whose image is on the coin?* They answered, *Caesar's.* Jesus responded, *Then, render to Caesar the things that are Caesar's and to God the things that are God's.*

What is Caesar to render to God? Whose image does Caesar bear? He was created in the image of God. Therefore, Caesar, just like every other individual on earth, including every elected official and all human institutions, must render to God what is due Him. And what is due God from Caesar, if God is supreme? Submission to God's authority, confession of God's supremacy and enforcement of God's law. For the civil government to do anything less is to resist God's order and to incur upon itself the judgment of God.

*To summarize: If God is supreme, we must submit to all His institutions. In addition, if He is supreme, all His institutions must submit to Him. They must recognize His supremacy and not the feigned supremacy of man. They must obey and enforce His will. Any political institution on earth, whether municipal, county, state or federal, that refuses to do so is at odds with God's order for creation and God will judge it for its irrational and inexcusable disobedience.*

James Henley Thornwell was a great Presbyterian preacher during the War Between the States. After the war was declared he plead with the Congress of the Confederacy to adopt the following amendment to her Constitution:

> We, the people of these Confederate States, distinctly acknowledge our responsibility to God and the supremacy of His Son, Jesus Christ, as King of kings and Lord of lords; and hereby ordain that no law shall be passed by the Congress of these Confederate States inconsistent with the will of God, as revealed in the Holy Scriptures.[1]

Nothing less than a similar, heart-felt confession today from the electorate and the elected officials will save this nation.

A controversial question waits to be asked: Is civil disobedience ever permissible for the Christian? The answer to that question must begin with a restatement of the citizen's God-given responsibility to submit to the governing authority of the state for God's sake. But that is not to say that if we ever break any civil law for any reason that we are sinning against God and that God will judge us for it. The Bible qualifies the nature and extent of our

---

1. *Presbyterian Heritage,* Vol. I, No. I, (Atlanta Christian Training Seminars)

submission to the civil government.

What if the civil government disregards God's supremacy and issues laws that are in conflict with those of God? What is the Christian's duty in that instance? If any political institution requires us to obey a civil law, compliance with which necessitates disobeying God's revealed law, we MUST disobey that civil law. We have no choice. God must be obeyed. We must disobey the state whenever it requires disobedience to God. If we obey the state at that point, we are in rebellion against God Himself. **Allegiance to God takes precedence over all other allegiances.**

In Exodus 1 we find that the state passed a law requiring infanticide for all male babies. In this situation we read about a group of godly Hebrew women who believed in the supremacy of Jehovah over the political powers of Egypt. When commanded by Pharaoh to commit murder, the godly midwives broke the law and deceived Pharaoh, for which God richly blessed them.

> The midwives feared God (not Pharaoh), and did not do as the king of Egypt had commanded them, but let the boys live ... So God was good to the midwives, and the people multiplied, and became very mighty (Exodus 1:17-20).

Daniel's example is also pertinent. The situation he lived through is very similar, though not identical, to the situation in which Christians find themselves in the United States in the 1990s — captivity of the Church in a humanistic culture and state.

Daniel treated his captors with respect, totalitarians though they were. He did not go out of his way to offend them. He did not use violence, civil rebellion, or non-cooperation to overturn them. He bent over backward to do everything he could so as not to offend them and to assist them in the effective administration of their nation. Yet, when they issued a regulation which outlawed public praying, Daniel did as he had always done. He broke the civil law, prayed as usual, and God preserved and blessed him for it.

Consider Shadrach, Meshach and Abednego. The Babylonian law required that all citizens bow before the image of Nebuchadnezzar, confessing his supremacy. Notice what these young men did in Daniel 3:16:

> Shadrach, Meshach, and Abednego answered and said to the king, "O, Nebuchadnezzar, we do not need to give you an answer concerning this. If it be so, our God whom we serve is able to deliver us from the furnace of blazing fire; and he will deliver us out of your hand, O king. But even if he does not, let it be known to you, O king, that we are not going to serve your gods or worship the golden image you have set up."

What faith and courage! Those three young men would not even eat the king's food in order to give testimony to the world that they would not be dependent upon the welfare of a totalitarian state. They refused the king and God kept them strong. They broke the civil law, capital offense though it was, because if they had not, they would have been guilty of breaking the first commandment.

In Acts 5 we find a municipal power issuing a law prohibiting the public preaching of the gospel within the city limits. The disciples of Jesus, knowing this law, nevertheless, stood on the "courthouse steps" and began preaching the gospel, thereby breaking the civil law. In Acts 5:28 the municipal authorities speak: *We gave you strict orders not to continue teaching in this name, and behold, you have filled Jerusalem with your teaching, and intend to bring this man's blood upon us.*

The point is clear: We may never break the law of God in order to obey the law of the state. The Hebrew midwives, Daniel, Shadrach, Meshach, Abednego, Peter and John were simply taking seriously the fact that God is supreme over all political institutions. It is a far more terrifying thing to fall into the hands of an angry God than to fall into the hands of an angry state.

CHAPTER TWO

# *The Function of Civil Government*

What did God institute civil government to do? Answer:

> For rulers are not a cause of fear for good behavior, but for evil. For it is a minister of God to you for good. But if you do what is evil, be afraid; for it does not bear the sword for nothing; for it is a minister of God, an avenger who brings wrath upon the one who practices evil (Romans13:3-4).

Here we have a clear statement in the New Testament of the God-appointed function of the civil government: *to terrorize evil doers.*

Before we consider further the biblical function of civil government, let us consider what functions God did *not* assign to civil government. Notice there is no mention in our passage about the responsibility for health, education or welfare. God has not assigned these responsibilities to the civil government. They belong to the individual, the family, the Church, and voluntary associations.

In the Old Testament we find that, in times of national emergency, the civil government may assist in the handling of plagues by assuring the merciful quarantine of the infectious for the protection of the healthy. In 1990 America is less healthy since the state has tried to control and improve our health.

The same is true of education. The Bible makes clear that it is the responsibility of parents (Deuteronomy 6:7f), with the assistance of the Church (Matthew 28:18f), to educate their children. Nowhere in the Bible does God give the civil government the authority or the competency to provide a general education for its citizens.

The Old Testament, however, does give the civil government the duty to educate the citizenry in the specific demands, prohibitions and sanctions of civil law (II Chronicles 17:9). King Jehoshaphat understood that a citizenry well-informed in its constitution and covenantal foundation was a strong citizenry, not easily swayed or intimidated. Since the civil government became involved in an attempt to provide and control education, Americans have become more ignorant, miseducated and illiterate.

And the same is true of welfare. The Bible does not give the civil government the responsibility to provide welfare and social security for its citizens. That vital responsibility has been given to the family, the diaconate of the Church and the community in voluntary (charitable) associations. In fact, America has become poorer since the civil government has tried to provide and control welfare.

What is the reason for this failure in providing welfare? In order for the state to provide welfare and security for one person, it must forcibly take security from someone else. In order to redistribute wealth to one person, it must confiscate the wealth of another person. There is no such thing as a free lunch!

The Constitution of the United States reflects this biblical political order. It states that the duty of the civil government is to "promote" the general welfare of all its citizens through the common defense, without patronizing any special interest groups, making sure that all our citizens are safe by defending them from criminals and subversives within our borders and from invaders and terrorists from without.

The U. S. Constitution does not give the federal government the responsibility for health, education or welfare, which means that the vast majority of the work of Congress today is unconstitutional and unbiblical.

What else does Romans 13 exclude from the proper functions of civil government? God has not given the state the responsibility to plan, regulate, and control people, property, contracts, schools, Churches, businesses and industry. The very idea that the state has this power to regulate and control implies that if there is no such planning by the state, there is no plan and no order at all in society. The state must become the predestining state, because there is no predestination, no order outside the state. This view of politics is an atheistic one. It denies one of the fundamental truths of the Bible: God is the great Predestinator (Isaiah 46:10-11). Life is governed by His plan. Submission to His supremacy and obedience to His law brings order, peace, freedom and prosperity to a society.

When the state regulates and controls, it squelches, impoverishes and enslaves. So the humanistic idea that the purpose of the state is to regulate and control everything, including the economy, rests on the anti-Christian principle that God is not in control of this world and that life does not move along according to the plan of God. It is a denial of the reality that voluntary submission of men and institutions to the regulative authority of God's Word secures liberty and justice for all.

What then is the function of civil government according to Romans 13:1-7? It is a singular duty: God has commissioned the civil government to protect law-abiding citizens by punishing evil doers, thereby maintaining God's law-order in a society.

Three biblical texts bear this out. Romans 13:3 says that *rulers are a terror to evil-doers.* I Timothy 2:1f says that *kings and all who are in authority* are to assure that a law-abiding person can *lead a tranquil and quiet life in all godliness and dignity.* In I Peter 2:13f we are commanded:

> Submit yourselves for the Lord's sake to every human institution, whether to a king as the one in authority, or to governors as sent by him for the punishment of evildoers and the praise of those who do right.

The biblical function of the state, then, is to terrorize evil doers and to punish all those who would hinder law-abiding citizens from living peaceful, quiet, godly, undisturbed, and dignified lives under God.

Imagine how small the budget of the civil government would be if it carried out this one and only biblical function! Imagine how small our tax bill would be! Imagine how safe we would be!

The names given to the civil government in Romans 13 reveal a great deal about its function and purpose. In verse one it is called *the governing authorities.* In verse three it is called a *ruler,* i.e., one whom God has placed in office and given the authority to govern.

In verse three it is also called a *terror to evil-doers,* i.e., it is to terrify those who do evil or who would do evil. If a state does not terrorize evil-doers by the enforcement of God's law, the state and society will be terrorized by evil-doers, as we have today.

In verse four the state is called a *minister of God* who is to act as God's *avenger* to bring God's *wrath upon the one who practices evil.* In the light of these designations, the purpose of the state is to avenge the supremacy of God towards rebels against God's order. And in verse six these rulers are called *the servants of God.* The state is to protect man by serving God.

All these names are given to the state by God to impress us with its responsibility of protecting us from lawbreakers by being a terror to those who break God's law and by being a servant of God which carries out His revealed will. In other words, the purpose of civil government is retribution or restitution. It is to make sure that God's justice is duly honored, that any injury done is recompensed, and that criminals bear the full force of the law, receiving the punishment their crimes deserve.

The book of Deuteronomy says that the courts are never to show mercy to convicted criminals (Deuteronomy 19:18-21). When a criminal is convicted, he must suffer the full weight of punishment his crime deserves. Justice demands it.

The punishment must fit the crime. The courts may not show mercy. Judges have no option, if the courts are to be a real terror to evil-doers. Would-be criminals must be certain they will be punished if they commit a crime, if the state is to be a terror to them, and hence, a deterrent.

**Where the criminal is shown mercy, the victim of his crime loses mercy.** Mercy will be shown to either the offender or the victim. It is proper to show mercy to the victim, but, if mercy is shown to the offender by the court, the victim is wronged and suffers twice. For example, if a convicted murderer is given a life sentence rather than execution, the taxes of law-abiding citizens, including the victim's family, will pay for his upkeep.

Moreover, the purpose of the courts of the land is not marriage counseling, social change or the rehabilitation of the criminal. The Bible is unmistakably clear in spelling out the single duty of courts: *Justice, and only justice, you shall pursue...* Deuteronomy 16:20. When a judge loses sight of this goal and moves into the realm of affecting social change by his decisions, then justice is perverted and liberty disappears.

A famous federal judge was asked to describe the make-up of the modern federal judiciary. He answered that there are two kinds of federal judges today: One is the judge who sees himself as the agent of immediate social transformation and the other is the judge who sees himself as having such a responsibility, but mildly so. In other words, there is only one kind of federal judge in America today, with a few exceptions: one who sees himself as an agent of social change (in a left-ward direction).

The only difference between them is that some are more zealous and more consistent than others. As far as the Bible is concerned, any judge who does not see himself as a champion of God's revealed law, whose duty is to administer God's justice, is a cruel and unjust hatchetman for the humanistic status quo, and is to be despised by lovers of liberty and justice.

The view that the purpose of the court is to rehabilitate the criminal is based on the old heresy of salvation by law(s) instead of by grace through faith in Christ. Law cannot rehabilitate, as more and more studies in criminal justice confirm. Neither the passing of laws nor the enforcing of laws can make a bad man good or a good man better. Only the gospel of Jesus Christ can do that. The purpose of the court, and civil government, is to restrain evil, not to change men.

In carrying out this retributive function, the civil government is to be concerned with actions, not thoughts or beliefs, privately held. It is not to try to control our thoughts or faith, or to bring our thoughts into conformity with "public policy."

In verse three, the state is said to be a terror for *evil behavior,* not evil thoughts. Also in verse three we are told to *do what is good* ... And in verse four we are warned that if we *do what is evil,* we should be afraid; and that God's wrath is administered by the state on those *who practice evil.* The point is that only God can judge the heart, and He does.

The purpose of civil government, then, is not to judge opinion. It is not to judge the heart. It is not to control thinking. Its concern is to judge actions, outward behavior and practices. The state should not be concerned with thought control, but with the control of lawless actions and with the judging of lawless behavior. And whenever it does that justly, it is acting as God's agent and God's representative. It becomes the minister of God.

In Romans 12:19, God says: *Vengeance is mine, I will repay.* Vengeance is God's personal prerogative. He is the only one who may execute vengeance. But here in Romans 13:4 we find that the civil government is *an avenger who brings* (divine) *wrath on the one who practices evil.* Vengeance belongs to God, but to a godly state God has given the authority to administer His vengeance. Whenever a civil government justly punishes a criminal, it is God acting through it. It bestows God's wrath.

God places "the sword" in the hands of the state, which uses it in His name. So then, when the civil government is acting properly and biblically, when it is not being swept off its feet by socialism, welfarism or pragmatism, when it is upholding God's revealed moral order, it is the official representative of Almighty God. When it administers sanctions and punishments on criminals, it is God administering those sanctions.

This is the reason the Bible says that if the civil government does not execute those who are deserving of capital punishment, God will bring His capital punishment to bear upon that whole society. God will have His vengeance!

If a state does not see itself as the one responsible to protect us by administering God's justice and God's wrath upon evil-doers, then the Bible says that God Himself will carry out that function and bring His own terrifying death penalty upon that nation. God will have His way (Deuteronomy 28).

God will vindicate His name and His moral order. He will execute His holy vengeance upon individuals and institutions which disobey Him. By means of a godly civil government, God acts, God judges, God protects, and God avenges. Hence, the state is the "servant" and "minister" of God, representing Him and His moral order.

The obvious implication of this is that **a civil government cannot be religiously neutral.** It may not be and it cannot be religiously neutral. In addressing judges God says:

> You shall not plant for yourself an Asherah (i.e., a wooden symbol of a female deity), or any kind of tree beside the altar of the Lord ... Neither shall you set up for yourself a sacred pillar which the Lord your God hates (Deuteronomy 16:21f).

How can the state be religiously neutral if it is instituted by the God of the Bible to be His servant, His minister, His representative to act in His name, to enforce His law, administer His wrath, endowed with His authority to maintain His moral order on earth?!

If the state does all this faithfully, it is favoring Christianity. If it does anything less or anything else, it is favoring anti-Christianity. It is impossible for a state not to favor some religion. A state is an idolatrous state under divine judgment if it favors any other god than the triune God of the Bible, and any other religion than biblical Christianity.

Religious commitments and perspectives about life are inescapable. They shape and color everything we do. What we believe about life at the deepest levels of our being will affect everything we do and every opinion we hold, including our political perspectives. We cannot escape our religion. Everyone has one. The question is, which religion does one hold — Christianity or Humanism, i.e., anti-Christianity? Just as an individual cannot escape his religious presuppositions, neither can a civil government escape favoring one religion over another.

America was founded as a nation favoring orthodox Christianity. B. F. Morris wrote in his 800 page book, *The Christian Life and Character of The Civil Institutions of The United States* (1863):

> The story of Christianity in America is one of the most astonishing chapters in the annals of the world. The events of Providence in reserving and preparing the country of these United States to be the theater of

its development and triumph, constitute one of the most remarkable passages of modern history.

This is a Christian nation, first in name, and secondly because of the many and mighty elements of a pure Christianity which have given it character and shaped its destiny from the beginning. It is preeminently the land of the Bible, of the Christian Church, and of the Christian Sabbath. The chief security and glory of the United States of America has been, is now, and will be forever, the prevalence and domination of the Christian Faith.

The purpose of the First Amendment to the Constitution is not to secularize or de-Christianize the government of the United States. That was never the intent of the authors of that Amendment. This secular view is superimposed on the Constitution by those whose agenda is the de-Christianization of America's civil and social institutions. U. S. Supreme Court Justice Joseph Story (1811-1845), refuted this secular approach to the First Amendment when he wrote:

> Probably at the time of the adoption of the Constitution, and of the first amendment to it ... the general, if not the universal, sentiment in America was that Christianity ought to receive encouragement from the state so far as was not incompatible with the private rights of conscience and the freedom of religious worship. Any attempt to level all religions, and to make it a matter of state policy to hold all in utter indifference, would have created universal disapprobation, if not universal indignation ... The real object of the amendment was not to countenance, much less to advance, Mahometanism, or Judaism, or infidelity, by prostrating Christianity; but to exclude all rivalry among Christian sects, and to prevent any national

ecclesiastical establishment which should give to a hierarchy the exclusive patronage of the national government.[1]

Religion will dominate politics and political institutions. The issue is not *whether* religion will influence politics, but *which* religion will influence politics — Christianity or humanism. If the civil government of the United States is to serve as a *minister of God* and thereby preserve liberty and justice for all, it must be Christianized institutionally, i.e., biblical truths must be allowed to give shape and content to our political institutions. This does not at all mean that some Christian denomination should be set up as the state Church which everyone must support by taxation. America is not Iran. The Bible is not the Koran. And Christianity is not Islam. But we *do* want the civil government of our land to favor Christianity again. We want it to stop favoring humanism, i.e., anti-Christianity, as it is presently doing, especially in the public (government) school system.

Humanism leads to the death of mankind. It leads to the murder of 20 million unborn babies in fifteen years by abortion. It leads to plague proportions of venereal diseases and AIDS. When a nation favors humanism, that nation will perish, unless it repents. In a humanistic nation, millions of people die of disease, drought, abortions, euthanasia, infanticide, unjust wars, terrorism, murder and suicide in

1. Whitehead, John., *The Second American Revolution* David C. Cook Publishing Co., 1982, Elgin, Ill. pp. 97-98.

fulfillment of Deuteronomy 28 and Leviticus 26.

At the heart of our political, economic, social and moral problems as a nation is our attempt to break free from our biblical roots, to break free from the claims that the supreme God has placed upon us. And as a just consequence, God is beginning to judge our land (Isaiah 3). The wages of sin are still death! Psalm 2 is still true!

What happens when a nation is faithful to God? What happens when a civil government genuinely confesses that God is supreme in the full sense of the word? The answer is found in Proverbs 20:2 *The terror of a* (godly) *king is like the growling of a lion; he who provokes him to anger forfeits his own life.* How different Atlanta, Georgia and Washington, D.C. would be if, when lawlessness occurred in those cities, the lion of the civil government would growl so ferociously that it would strike terror in the hearts of criminals who assault the moral order of God.

Proverbs 20:8 says, *A king who sits on the throne of justice disperses all evil with his eyes.* This godly king who administers God's justice is such a terrifying sight when he is enraged by lawlessness that, when a criminal merely sees the look in his eye, it horrifies and deters him. That is the kind of civil government that pleases God.

However, if it uses deadly force to impose any other system of justice than that of the Bible it will terrify the righteous. The criminal, not the godly citizen, shall tremble at the sight of a policeman, soldier, governor or president. In a truly Christian state, the godly citizen can look at these men with a smile of respect and appreciation. But when the lawless person looks at these political authorities he should tremble because he knows that this civil government is committed to maintaining the peace, preserving justice, and that those who provoke this "king" by their acts of lawlessness forfeit their lives.

If the United States government were to do as God commands, it would seek to preserve His moral order, His peace, His justice, and, in so doing, it would protect the godly. Liberty and justice for all would abound. There would be an environment conducive to the spread of the gospel by the Church.

The Christian community would be able to develop and blossom in its business without any restraints by the state on its schools, homes, property, vocations, and economic development. We would see the kingdom of Christ capture and transform more and more areas of American culture as Christians worked to reconstruct by the Word of God more and more American institutions in education, economics, law, media, medicine, and technology.

We would begin to see in our hearts and society the will of God done on earth as it is in heaven. Pray that that day will come in our generation. Work toward that great objective: the Christianization of every facet of American society and culture and the evangelization of every American citizen and family.

When that day comes, you and I will be able to

spend all our days working hard in our callings, worshipping God with our families in our churches, earning what we deserve, keeping what we make, spending like we want, being able to tithe, doing on our property what we desire and what is pleasing to God, and educating our children in the way we think they should be educated. We would have a strong, secure, prosperous, free, just and godly nation blessed by Almighty God.

As the civil government preserves order in a society by maintaining God's moral order by His standard of justice, the Church can work at saving that society by the propagating of the gospel of Jesus Christ in the power of the Holy Spirit. Both of these institutions, Church and State, must maintain God's order for a society thereby restraining lawlessness in that society. When a godly order is maintained, the Church then has the room and freedom to carry out the mandate God has given it to make the nations of the world Christ's disciples.

Think hard on these powerful words by A. A. Hodge, a Presbyterian preacher of the last century:

> If Christ is really king, exercising original and immediate jurisdiction over the state as really as he does over the Church, it follows necessarily that the general denial or neglect of His rightful lordship, any prevalent refusal to obey that Bible which is the open law-book of His kingdom, must be followed by political and social as well as moral and religious ruin.
>
> If professing Christians are unfaithful to the authority of their Lord in their capacity as citizens of the state, they cannot expect to be blessed by the indwelling of the Holy Spirit in their capacity as members of

the Church. The kingdom of Christ is one and cannot
be divided in life or in death.

If the Church languishes, the state cannot be in
health, and if the state rebels against its Lord and
King, the Church cannot enjoy His favor. If the Holy
Spirit is withdrawn from the Church He is not present
in the state, and if He, the only Lord and Giver of Life,
be absent, then all order is impossible and the elements of society lapse backward to primeval night and
chaos.

In the name of your own interests I plead with you;
in the name of your treasure-houses and barns; of your
rich farms and cities; of your accumulations in the
past and your hopes in the future I charge you — you
never will be secure if you do not faithfully maintain
all the crown-rights of Jesus the King of men.

In the name of your children and their inheritance
of the precious Christian civilization you in turn have
received from your sires; in the name of the Christian
Church, I charge you that its sacred franchise, religious liberty, cannot be retained by men who in civil
matters deny their allegiance to the King. In the name
of your own soul and its salvation; in the name of the
adorable Victim of that bloody and agonizing sacrifice
whence you draw all your hopes of salvation; by
Gethsemane and Calvary; I charge you, citizens of the
United States, afloat on your wide sea of politics,
*There is another King, one Jesus: The safety of the state
can be secured only in the way of humble and whole-
souled loyalty to His Person and of obedience to His
law.*[2]

---

2. Hodge, A. A., *Popular Lectures On Theological Themes,* Presbyterian Board of Education, 1887, Philadelphia, pp. 285-287.

CHAPTER THREE

# The Power of a Minister of God

God has given the civil government three powers so that it can be effective in carrying out its responsibility to maintain His moral order. These three powers, mentioned in Romans 13:1-7, are: (1) the power of a minister of God; (2) the power of the sword; and (3) the power to tax. We will deal with each in the next three chapters.

The first power God has given the state is the power of a minister of God. Faithful use of this power makes the state a real terror to evil-doers. In Romans 13:4 the state is twice called a *minister of God.*

When the state acts as such it promotes the welfare, security and happiness of law-abiding citizens. But, if a person commits lawless acts, that same minister-servant of God has the power and authority to bestow God's wrath on that person in order to stop his assault on God's moral order and his disturbance of a peaceful society.

The state is enabled to do this as a minister of God as it enforces biblical law. It has the ministerial power and responsibility to differentiate biblically between right and wrong to punish the wrong and to honor the right.

The state's authority is "ministerial." It has an authority in the civil sphere similar to that of the minister-preacher in the ecclesiastical sphere. Both elected politicians and preachers are called *ministers of God* in the Bible. Each has different responsibilities and official duties, but a similar kind of authority. Both have ministerial authority but not legislative authority.

The preacher has not been given the legislative authority to create new doctrines and legislate new ethics by fiat "ex nihilo." He is called by God to administer the gospel he finds written in the Bible, without subtraction or addition.

Some preachers are creators of new doctrines, but in so doing they have over-stepped the boundaries of their authority and have renounced God's supremacy over them. The true preacher is to administer biblical truth in his preaching and teaching. He is a *minister* of truth, he is not a *source* of truth.

The same is true of the state. Its authority is ministerial not legislative. God has not given it the right to create laws, legislation, and policies by fiat *ex nihilo*. It may not invent regulations based on the latest opinion poll or the most recent expert advice. The state may administer and apply to our modern situation the laws it finds written in the Bible governing the civil sphere.

It is the minister of law and justice, not the source of either. The state is not the minister of man, nor of the majority, nor of the powerful. It is the minister of God. It represents God. It stands for His moral order, therefore, it may legislate only those laws that are true applications of the biblical law of Almighty God.

To say that we need additional, extra-biblical, or contra-biblical laws, to satisfy the needs of our modern age is to deny the Bible's all-sufficient, eternal authority for all of life in all ages (Deuteronomy 4:1f; 8:12-32; 29:29). The Bible tells us everything we need to know to be thoroughly equipped to maintain a well-ordered society, because the Bible is not the word of man, nor the word of the state, it is the eternal Word of God written.

God has given the civil government, as the minister of God, the authority to obey and enforce biblical law. He has not given it the authority to do anything else or anything less. If it does anything other than obeying and enforcing biblical law, it is usurping authority God has not given it. Therefore it becomes obvious that this God-given power is also a God-given limitation on the state's power. Transgression of that limitation brings God's judgment.

To put it another way, the state is involved in issues pertaining to good and evil, right and wrong. However, some people want the state to take a "neutral" posture regarding moral issues, and to be concerned simply with political issues. They say, "Morality is for the Church. Let's keep it out of politics."

There are two serious problems with that viewpoint:

(1) It is impossible to separate morality, religion and politics. George Washington saw this clearly when he said in his Farewell Address:

> Of ... all the dispositions and habits which lead to political prosperity, religion and morality are indispensable supports. In vain would that man claim the tribute of patriotism, who should labor to subvert

> these great pillars of human happiness, these firmest props of the duties of men and citizens. — And let us with caution indulge the supposition that morality can be maintained without religion. Whatever may be conceded to the influence of refined education on minds of peculiar structure, reason and experience both forbid us to expect that national morality can prevail in exclusion of religious principle ... virtue or morality is a necessary spring of popular government.

When Washington spoke of religion, he meant the Christian religion, as John Eidsmoe documents in his book, *Christianity And The Constitution* (Baker Book House, 1987, Grand Rapids, MI., pp. 113-143).

(2) Romans 13:3-4 does not allow for any dichotomy between morality and politics:

> For rulers are not a cause of fear for good behavior, but for evil. Do you want to have no fear of authority? Do what is good, and you will have praise from the same ... for it is a minister of God to you for good. But if you do what is evil, be afraid; for it does not bear the sword for nothing; for it is a minister of God, an avenger who brings wrath upon the one who practices evil.

Political institutions, by their very nature, are intimately involved in issues of good and evil. They are inescapably concerned with morality and behavior. In fact, there is not one political issue that is not at heart a moral issue. Abortion is a political and a moral problem. The murder of unborn people is evil.

Taxation, inflation and welfarism are political and moral issues. To use political power to take the property of one and give it to another is theft. It is legal plunder.

National defense issues (viz. treaties, SDI, free-dom-fighter aid) are political and moral issues. Are American families to be left defenseless in the face of the largest military build-up in history in the U.S.S.R., which remains devoted to the defeat of the West regardless of the mask of glasnost? Is our defense strategy based on retaliation (Mutual Assured Destruction), or a defense that actually defends (SDI and Mutual Assured Survival)? These are moral issues.

The point is that regardless of the nature of the political issue, it is concerned with right and wrong, good and evil, morality and immorality. So in this sense, it is the responsibility of the state to legislate biblical morality. We must not flinch at this point. For a nation to remain free and just, its civil government must enforce biblical law.

Is the state really to "legislate morality?" It all depends on what is meant by that phrase. If legislating morality refers to the effort to make people good by passing laws, then, of course, as Christians, we must take issue with that view. Christians believe that only Jesus Christ can save sinners. Only He can make people good.

Humanists, on the other hand, do believe that the state can make people good by passing laws. They believe, for instance, that, if guns are banned, there will be less crime. But guns do not cause crime. Bad people cause crime. Banning guns will not make bad people better. "Guns cause crime like flies cause garbage."

In what sense, then, is the state to legislate morality? In this sense: every piece of legislation represents someone's understanding of right and wrong. Whose understanding, whose standards are we going to allow to determine the direction of legislation in the United States: the standards of man or the revealed standards of God?

The purpose of the civil government is to make sure that God's system of public morality is firmly established and maintained in a culture, because if God's law does not remain at the foundation of a nation's life, that nation will not last long. So, we have a choice. We either can have a Christian society where God's law governs everything and where it is the purpose of the state to obey and enforce that law, or we can have a humanistic, anti-Christian state.

The first protects and enhances life and liberty. One might say that it is an exaggeration to say that humanism produces bloody cultures, but twenty million brutally aborted babies say it is not an exaggeration!

The legislation of Christian public morality pre-serves liberty and justice for all. The legislation of humanistic public (im)morality destroys them both, because humanism calls good what God calls evil. And evil is opposed to everything God is and every-thing man is and should be.

It might sound peculiar to some to hear that the civil government's responsibility is to obey and enforce biblical law. It sounds so archaic, so legalistic. It would be archaic, and even stupid, if the moral and civil laws of the Bible originated with man and were useful only in a primitive, agrarian, Hebrew culture. But the Bible is the Word of the Eternal God and it *endures forever.*

The Bible is true and applicable in all ages, precisely because it is the written revelation of God. And as for biblical law being "legalistic," compare the few hundred laws of the Bible with the thousands upon thousands of new laws and regulations passed by Congress every year. Add to that the thousands of annual executive orders and policies of the presidency. Count the pages of the Federal Register.

It is not biblical law that is "legalistic" and restricting, it is humanistic, statist law, all of which is unjust and restrictive on our lives, liberty, businesses and property. If the federal government were to annul all of the laws legislated in the past one hundred years and pass into law the few hundred moral laws of the Bible, this country would have more freedom, strength, security, prosperity, justice, righteousness, love and happiness than it has ever had in its history. Of course, this won't happen until the hearts of Americans are converted to Jesus Christ.

A Christian Republic has far fewer laws, far fewer government employees, and is far less expensive than any humanistic democracy, i.e., socialistic state (II Chronicles 12:8). Humanism in control of our federal government is bankrupting America.

Israel was commanded to obey and enforce God's law in the political arena. In II Chronicles 34:31 we read:

> Then the king stood in his place and made a covenant before the Lord to walk after the Lord, and to keep his commandments and his testimonies and his statutes with all his heart and with all his soul, to perform the words of the covenant written in this book.

We must earnestly pray that the next time the President of the United States is sworn into office, when he places his hand on the Bible, he will say: "I do hereby covenant before God to walk and rule in terms of His statutes and testimonies with all my heart and soul." When a President places his hand on the Bible, and does not make this covenant with God, he is a hypocrite and not worthy of that high office.

Throughout Israel's life her political leaders were held responsible by God to enforce God's law and to maintain His moral order over against all others. In Ezekiel 44:24, God says to political powers:

> And in a dispute they shall take their stand to judge; they shall judge it according to my ordinances. They shall also keep my laws and my statutes in all my appointed feasts, and sanctify my Sabbath.

Israel's prophets could not conceive of an orderly, just and free society unless the political leaders were committed to obeying and enforcing God's laws, and no other. Some people would attempt to refute the force of this argument by saying that, while this might have been expected of Israel, it was not expected of the non-Israeli nations of the Old Testament. This view is easily shown to be in error. In the Old Testament God was as demanding on the other nations of the world, as He was on Israel. Isaiah 13-23 and Jeremiah 45-51 vividly describe God's judgment on Babylon, Assyria, Egypt, Edom, Moab and various other nations of the world because they would not obey and enforce biblical law.

Proverbs 14:34 says: *Righteousness* (i.e., conformity to God's law), *exalts a nation, but sin* (i.e., transgression of God's law), *is a disgrace to any people.* Any nation that lives in conformity to God's revealed Word will be exalted by God; and any nation that neglects or denies that Divine Word will be disgraced by God. Psalm 2:10f drives this point home when it addresses all the earth's judges and political leaders:

> Now therefore, O kings, show discernment; take warning, O judges of the earth. Serve the Lord with reverence, and rejoice with trembling. Do homage to the Son, lest he become angry, and you perish in the way....

The same point is made in Leviticus 18:24-28:

> Do not defile yourselves by any of these things; for by all these the nations which I am casting out before you have become defiled. For the land has become defiled, therefore I have visited its punishment upon it, so the land has spewed out its inhabitants. But as for you, you are to keep my statutes and my judgments, and shall not do any of these abominations,

neither the native, nor the alien who sojourns among
you; (for the men of the land who have been before you
have done all these abominations, and the land has
become defiled); so that the land may not spew you out,
should you defile it, as it has spewed out the nation
which has been before you.

When Israel entered the land of Canaan, it entered a vicinity full of non-Israeli, non-"Christian,"
idolatrous nations. God judged those nations precisely because they defiled the land with abomi-
nable disobedience to His laws. So, whether it is
Israel or Gentile nations, all political institutions
throughout the world are responsible to God to obey
and enforce His law. To do anything else is to bring
God's judgment on that culture.

Romans 13:1-7 presents us with a genuine covenant relationship. A Christian Republic is based on
a three-fold covenant: (1) The covenant the citizenry
makes with God when it says: "We do hereby commit ourselves to be governed entirely by the Word of
God." (2) The covenant between the state and God,
wherein the head of state says: "I promise that I will
rule exclusively in terms of the law of Almighty
God." (3) The covenant between the state and the
citizenry, wherein they bind themselves together:
the state promising to administer God's justice on
their behalf, and the people promising to obey the
state as long as it is faithful to its covenant obliga-
tions (Joshua 1:17).

There is an increasing totalitarianism on the part
of the federal government, state governments,
county governments, and city governments in our

country, which is inevitable when a nation rejects God's law as the basis of its life and order. Tyranny is a political order wherein the final source of law, the final standard of right and wrong, is man or the political order itself.

For many, whatever the Supreme Court says is legal is moral. Some have even gone so far as to say that they once believed that abortion was wrong until the Supreme Court made it legal. Such a person is a slave and that mentality breeds totalitarianism.

Free nations are nations that take their definition of good and evil from God's law, not from human subjectivity or the goals of the state. Critics would say, "What you are proposing sounds like a Theocracy." The word, theocracy, has a variety of meanings and connotations. Theocracies like that of the totalitarian Islamic regime of Ayatollah Khomeini's Iran are repulsive to all lovers of truth, freedom and justice. In truth, that is not a theocracy but a dictatorship.

Many people think a theocracy is a political order governed dictatorially by Church leaders, simply by virtue of the fact that they are Church leaders. But, the Bible does not teach that the state should be subjected to the Church any more than the Church should be subjected to the state.

Theocracy is a very proper description of a godly political order, when that word is defined correctly. Israel in the Old Testament was a true and wholesome theocracy, and it also had a clear institutional and functional separation of Church and state. Neither Church nor state was totalitarian.

A theocracy, in the biblical sense of the word, is a nation where God's revealed law is supreme over all human laws, and is the source of all laws.

A label describing such an order that could be substituted for theocracy is Christian Republic. Israel in the Old Testament had a constitutional republic. In its better days, it was a republic, governed by elected representatives, where God's law was the basis for its constitutional and covenantal union (confederacy). Israel was to be a holy nation, where God reigned through His representatives, who faithfully executed His law. And where God reigns, there freedom, justice, strength, peace, and prosperity abound.

E. C. Wines refers to the theocracy of the Old Testament as "The Hebrew Republic," in his book by the same name. He shows how the origin of this American Republic is not in Greece or Rome, but in the theocratic laws of Moses. He writes:

> Such, then, as I conceive, were the great ideas, the fundamental principles, which lay at the basis of the Hebrew state. The unity of God, the unity of the nation, civil liberty, political equality, an elective magistracy, the sovereignty of the people, the responsibility of public officers to their constituents, a prompt, cheap and impartial administration of justice, peace and friendship with other nations, agriculture, universal industry, the inviolability of private property, the sacredness of the family relation, the sanctity of human life, universal education, social union, a well-adjusted balance of powers, and an

> enlightened, dignified, venerable public opinion, were
> the vital elements of the constitution of Moses.[1]

If a civil government refuses to obey and enforce God's revealed laws, it degenerates into a minister of Satan. A Russian Baptist preacher who spent six years in a Siberian labor camp was asked how he interpreted Romans 13:1. His answer was: "I'll tell you how every true Christian in Russia understands Romans 13:1. We understand it to say that the governmental authority is ordained of God to do the will of God, but when the government denies the existence of God and persecutes the people of God, it is not of God, but of the devil."

He understands Romans 13 better than many Americans, and much better than all those German Christians who sold out to the Nazis under Hitler. When the state turns to another law-order than that of the Bible, it ceases being the minister of God and becomes the minister of Satan. As Christians, we may never give unqualified obedience or allegiance to such a civil government. In fact, we must diligently work against its efforts to rid itself of Christianity. Our allegiance to Jesus Christ always defines the nature and extent of our submission to the state.

The Bible describes such an anti-Christian state as a terrifying, murderous "Beast" (Revelation 13). In Revelation 13, the civil government, which God

1. Wines, E. C., *The Hebrew Republic,* The American Presbyterian Press, Oxbridge, Mass., p. 63.

gave to promote His peace and justice, is said to be a hideous, frightening, terrorizing Beast which rips and tears its citizens.

When does the state become this Beast? When does the state cease being a minister of God and become a minister of Satan? It does so when it terrorizes Christians, when it brings vengeance upon Christians, rather than upon the lawless. What would make a civil government do that? When does it turn beastly? Answer: when a civil government denies, neglects or repudiates its responsibility to obey and enforce biblical law, it becomes the cruel, beastly enemy of its law-abiding citizens, terrorizing them and their children.

Has the federal government of the United States become the enemy of its godly citizens? It has become a "terrorist state" against its citizens by threatening our liberty, prosperity, security, and our very lives; because it has clearly turned its back on its accountability to the supremacy of Almighty God.

What happens when a state becomes a Beast? What happens when it no longer enforces God's law, but commits itself to a humanistic, anti-Christian, satanic law-order? Liberty and justice for all are redefined into meaninglessness. Peace disappears. Prosperity shrivels. Twenty million babies are aborted. Churches and Christian schools are persecuted.

Christians are the first to suffer, because Christians, who take God's Word seriously, are always the biggest threat to any state that thinks it is God. Christians are viewed by the Beast as the real terrorists and as fanatical extremists. This is why ancient Rome fed the Christians to the lions. It was not because they worshipped Jesus. It was because they worshipped *only* Jesus, and not Caesar. They would not prostitute their allegiance to Jesus Christ.

They would not bow before any authority governing their lives except the authority of the Lord Jesus Christ. This is why, when a state becomes a Beast, apostatizing from its biblical base, Christian homes, individuals, churches, schools, and organizations are the first to be persecuted or discredited. It is the Christians who will be terrorized and penalized the most severely, along with others, with high taxes, inflation, bureaucratic regulations, false charges and imprisonment, while the lawless are protected and well cared for.

Everything is turned upside down in a state that has become a Beast. So, in terms of the Bible, we are faced with those who bear the mark of the Beast (Revelation 13:17), versus those who bear the seal of God (Revelation 14:1,12). The sides are drawn. The Bible says in Revelation that the Beast has a mark which it places in the forehead and on the hand of its slaves. Unless a person bears that mark he cannot carry on any commerce, but he will become an outcast to his society.

Over against the Beast and those whom he brands as his own are those who belong exclusively and totally to God, who bear His brand in their foreheads and hands. To what does this have reference? What is this "mark" and this "seal"?

Deuteronomy is the key to understanding these figures. In Deuteronomy God tells His people, in figurative terms, to put His law on their foreheads, hands, doorposts, mouths and hearts (Deuteronomy 6:8f).

They are to keep the law of God before their eyes, in their minds, and on their hands, because it is only as they live in glad submission to that law for Jesus' sake that they are a free and blessed people. So, in Revelation, the mark of the Beast is not a plastic credit card and the Beast is not a giant computer in Belgium.

To bear the mark of the Beast is to surrender to another law-order than that of the Bible. The person who wears the mark of the Beast in his forehead and hand is a person who lives in terms of the totalitarian laws of man and Satan, instead of the perfect and liberating laws of God (James 1:25). He is the person who refuses to govern his own thoughts and life by the Bible, choosing instead to submit himself to the anti-Christian, beastly dictates of the judicial decisions, legislation, regulations, and public policies of the Beast.

Who is the person who bears the seal of God? It is that man, woman or young person who has God's law written in his head, heart and hands. For that person, who is a believer in Jesus, biblical law is the regulating principle of the entirety of his life. He works to overturn the plots and schemes of the

Beast, and to restore his state to its foundation in the Word of God. Those who bear the mark of the Beast will be rewarded and defrauded by the Beast. They will also be cursed by God. Those who bear the seal of God will be persecuted by the Beast, but they will be rewarded and protected by God. And eventually, they will triumph over the Beast. Praise God!

There is a war in the United States between those in political power and their "useful idiots" who bear the mark of the Beast, and who are committed to a humanistic law-order versus those who bear the seal of God and who are committed to the law-order of Jesus Christ revealed in the Old and New Testaments. In this war, the Beast must be resisted by the Bride. If the Bride of Christ does not resist the Beast, no one else will, because no one else has the power to kill the Beast.

Mere political conservatives do not have the power to resist the Beast. Merely conservative political action groups do not have the power to do it. They are important in their places, but there is only one force in the United States powerful enough to stop the terrorism of the Beast dead in its tracks: the Church of the Lord Jesus Christ using the Sword of the Spirit, which is the Word of God (Ephesians 6:17; II Corinthians 10:4).

When a political ruler violates his covenant with God and no longer obeys or enforces God's law, he has forfeited his right to govern. When a political ruler has forfeited his right to govern, it is the duty of Christians to resist him and to remove him from office. When we fail to do so, when we fail to oppose the Beast with biblical methods and strategies, we become accomplices of his crime, and God will punish us and the entire nation for our silence, cowardice, and complicity.

Simply going along, pacifying the Beast, not opposing and resisting the enemy of liberty and justice, of God and of our children, is a suicidal sin. The Beast must be resisted by the Bride with the Sword of the Word of God, and *only the Sword of the Word of God*, in her hand.

Only you and I, as the Church of Jesus Christ, have the power to stop the Beast in America and the world. If we do not start plunging the Sword of the Spirit into the heart of its leaders and institutions, it will soon gobble up our children.

CHAPTER FOUR

# *The Power of the Sword*

This God-given power of the state is mentioned in. Romans 13:4: *...for it is a minister of God to you for good. But if you do what is evil, be afraid; for it does not bear the sword for nothing.* What *is* this power of the sword? What is its purpose? How is it used for nothing?

A metal sword is not used to butter bread. The "sword" represents the use of legal force, and when necessary, of deadly force, by the state in order to carry out its God-defined function. God Himself has given the civil government the authority to use legal (deadly) force in order to enforce His law and protect the law-abiding from the lawless.

God places the sword in the hand of the state and says to it: "Use this according to my definition of right and wrong to maintain my moral order and to protect law-abiding citizens." The sword, then, stands for coercion. Therefore, in order to administer justice and keep the peace, the state has been given the power of coercion in the suppression of lawlessness.

It is an inescapable duty in a fallen world. When a civil government surrenders that responsibility, the lawless will suppress and coerce the law-abiding. When a nation refuses to suppress lawless acts, as defined by the Bible (because only the Creator can define what is lawless and lawful), it is the law-abiding citizen who is suppressed and terrorized, as lawlessness reigns supreme.

The reason the state must often use legal coercion

to maintain God's moral order is that the only way lawless people will be restrained from lawless acts is by coercing them by legal, sometimes deadly, force to stop their lawless activity. God has not given the state the power of the sword to convert the world to Christianity. Nor was the sword given for conquest. The purpose of the sword is not to conquer the world for America. That is the Islamic view of Gaddafi, Khomeini and Hussein, but it is anti-Christian.

The purpose of the sword can be defined in three ways. *First,* the purpose of the sword is to enable the state to protect the law-abiding from the lawless. If the state is going to provide this protection, it must have strength superior to that of the lawless. If someone seeks to do us harm with a machine gun, the state will be of no help at all if it only has a feather duster.

The godly state must be of superior strength to evil men and nations. This is the teaching of Jesus Himself:

> Or what king, when he sets out to meet another king in battle, will not first sit down and take counsel whether he is strong enough with ten thousand men to encounter the one coming against him with twenty thousand? (Luke 14:31).

*Second,* a Christian Republic with a sword in its hand is a holy terror to evil-doers. Romans 13:3 says just that: the power of the sword is to strike terror in the hearts of those who even contemplate breaking the law. When a civil government no longer strikes terror in the hearts of the lawless, it can no longer protect its law-abiding citizens from those who would do them harm.

*Third,* the power of the sword is to be used to administer God's justice, to make sure that God's order is maintained, and that restitution is made whenever God's law is broken. When crimes are committed against God's law, restitution must be made to God, to the society, and to the victim (or his family) of the crime, in order for peace and order to continue. The state's function is to punish wrongs committed and to right those wrongs.

The sword is to be used for that purpose: to punish the criminal and to assure the victim of restitution and compensation, which he deserves as a result of the injury done against him. Moreover, the sword is to be used to satisfy God's justice and to vindicate His creation order.

In our society today, more people are talking about the value of restitution, but few know what true restitution to the victim of a crime really is. Charging criminals fines to be paid to the court (the state) is not restitution. Restitution is to be made to the victim or his family.

In our culture it is not the victim that is protected and pitied, it is the criminal. For this reason the Bible instructs the judicial system not to show mercy to the criminal. It does not have the option to pardon him for crimes committed. He must receive the punishment he deserves, if justice is to be done. Why? To show mercy to the criminal is to show no mercy to the victim.

In a major American city recently, a preacher's daughter was brutally raped, tortured and murdered. Instead of receiving the death penalty as he deserved, the court sentenced the killer to life in prison. *The compassion of the wicked is cruel* (Proverbs 12:10). When God's law is rejected in the courts, the victim is the one who is brutalized. Who will pay now for the room and board (for life) of that young woman's murderer? It will be her parents, friends, and relatives — through taxation.

For the rest of the murderer's life in prison, the hard-earned money of the grief-stricken family of the victim will go toward the upkeep and comfort of the murderer. That is compassion? That is perversion!

## The Use of the Sword in Domestic Affairs

God has given the civil government the authority to use the sword to preserve justice in our domestic relationships with each other within a nation. But in order for that power to be used effectively, there are certain other things that must be in place as well. Without these other things in place and functioning properly, any attempt on the part of the state to administer the sword will be exaggerated and frustrating.

In order for the civil government to work effectively, the individual must function properly. The individual must be practicing self-government and self-discipline under the Word of God. There must be true love for neighbor which moves us to be watchful of our neighbor's welfare and protection.

If we see a weaker person being attacked or mistreated, we do not shut our eyes and walk away. We come to his assistance. The Bible teaches us that if we have the ability to stop a crime being perpetrated and we do nothing, we become accomplices to that crime (Deuteronomy 22:1f, 19:18f).

Without love for neighbor that causes us to look out for the interests and welfare of each other, the civil government will not be able to protect us. Along with neighborly love, there must be true love for the living God and His order for our lives. We must be devoted to it. We must endeavor to preserve it.

Without self-government, love for neighbor, and love for God and His revealed order, the state will not be able to stop crime.

The Church is also directly involved in the restraining of lawlessness in a society. It restrains lawlessness by Church discipline. The more the Church of Jesus Christ stands guard over its members, practices loving Church discipline, preaches and teaches the whole Word of God, and observes the sacraments, the more effective it will be in restraining crime. The more faithful and effective the Church becomes using "the keys of the kingdom," the more effective the state will become by "the power of the sword."

The family has a central role in restraining crime and lawlessness in a society. As parents begin to understand their responsibilities toward each other and toward their children, the more faithfully parents practice family discipline, and bring up their children as covenant children in the nurture and discipline of the Lord, the sooner crime will diminish in a community. As parents educate their children in Christian schools, instead of turning them over to crime-ridden, drug-filled, state-supported, humanistic schools, crime will decrease.

Parents restraining lawlessness in their homes, Churches restraining lawlessness in their congregations, and states restraining lawlessness in their jurisdiction is not enough. A society will always be crime-ridden unless it is dominated by the faith that man's evil character can only be reformed by the gospel of Jesus Christ.

Neither Church discipline nor civil sanctions have the power to change a person's fallen, evil character. The only way an individual can experience lasting and substantial change in the right direction, at the deepest levels of his life, is through the redemptive grace of God in Christ through faith. Unless a culture is dominated by that faith, it will never be protected from rampant lawlessness.

Many today are trying to restrain lawlessness, stop the drug traffic, end abortion, preserve justice in the courts, build up our national defense, and maintain the peace, without this one indispensable ingredient: Jesus Christ.

None of these endeavors will work unless we, as a nation, are motivated on the inside by the faith that it is only Christ who can save sinful persons and nations. As long as people look to the state, the family, the Church, the school, or to science and technology to rehabilitate and reform people from their evil ways, these people will get nowhere in protecting themselves from the rage of lawlessness.

The Church must do its part. The individual must do his/her part. And the family must do its part if the state is to be successful doing its part. Civil government is founded on self-government. In order for any of these institutions to act effectively, that whole society must be committed to the faith that Jesus Christ alone is the Savior of the world. *There is no other name under heaven that has been given among men, by which we must be saved* (Acts 4:12).

The domestic use of the sword includes the legitimacy of capital punishment. This is always a controversial subject. What does the Bible say about it? God says that the state is to use the sword to put to death those citizens under that government who have committed crimes deserving of death. Genesis 9, Exodus 13, and Romans 13 may all be used as our scriptural support for believing that "the power of the sword" includes the authority (and duty) to execute convicted capital criminals.

There are three fundamental reasons why capital punishment is essential to public justice: (1) the holy character of God; (2) the holy command of God; and (3) the sanctity (holiness) of human life, the family, and God's moral order.

**First, the holy character of God is the basis**

**of capital punishment.** God's character is of such a holy and righteous nature that it is moved to absolute repulsion and intolerance against anything that opposes it or contradicts it (Romans 1:18). In holy anger God is moved to destroy that which opposes Him (Joshua 7:1). If God did not punish evil in His creation, it would mean that He took lightly His own character as God and His own established order for creation.

The fact that God is holy and righteous, that He will not tolerate lawlessness, and that He seeks to punish it and to expunge it from societies by placing the sword in the hand of the state are foundational principles for our understanding of the legitimacy of capital punishment.

In Genesis 9 we are told that if one person murders another person, that person forfeits his own life. Therefore, the civil government has the duty to put murderers to death (Numbers 35:30f). Murder is not the only capital crime in the Bible (Matthew 15:4; Mark 7:10; Deuteronomy 24:7; Leviticus 20:10-21; Deuteronomy 22:23-27; Exodus 22:18; Deuteronomy 21:18-21; Leviticus 24:11-24; Exodus 35:2; Deuteronomy 13:1-10).

This biblical approach to capital punishment is reflected in America today. Between our various states there are several capital crimes on the books: murder, kidnapping, certain sex crimes, incorrigible criminality, to name a few. These are remnants of a Christian culture in our land.

When a civil government neglects or denies its responsibility to put to death capital criminals, crime soars. When the Supreme Court declared capital punishment unconstitutional, within one year the United States experienced more rapes and murders than it ever had in any previous year in its history. During the years in which capital punishment was outlawed, rape and murder doubled.

**Second, the holy command of God is the basis of capital punishment.** God commands the state to put to death criminals convicted of capital crimes. Numbers 35:30-33 declares:

> If anyone kills a person, the murderer shall be put to death at the evidence of two witnesses, but no person shall be put to death on the testimony of one witness. Moreover, you shall not take ransom for the life of a murderer who is guilty of death, but he shall surely be put to death. And you shall not take ransom for him who has fled to his city of refuge, that he may return to live in the land before the death of the priest. So you shall not pollute the land in which you are; for blood pollutes the land and no expiation can be made for the land for the blood that is shed on it, except by the blood of him who shed it.

God says that capital crimes pollute the land and the only way of "un-polluting" it is by shedding the blood of the offender who committed the crime. How polluted is America!

Deuteronomy 19:18-21 says:

> And the judges shall investigate thoroughly; and if the witness is a false witness and he has accused his brother falsely, then you shall do to him just as he had intended to do to his brother. Thus you shall purge the evil from among you. And the rest will hear and be

afraid, and will never again do such an evil thing
among you. Thus you shall not show pity: life for life,
eye for eye, tooth for tooth, hand for hand, foot for foot.

Criminals must be punished justly, certainly,
swiftly and severely in order to purge evil from
society and to deter crime. The death penalty is a
deterrent to crime when it is administered biblically, publicly, swiftly and certainly. God says it is.

Furthermore, this text in Deuteronomy gives us
the principle by which a crime is determined to be a
capital offense: the heinousness of the crime determines the severity of the punishment. The punishment must always fit the crime.

**Third, the sanctity (holiness) of human life
and the family is the basis of capital punishment.** Capital criminals are to be executed by the
state because of the sanctity of human life and the
family. Since men and women are created in the
image of God, human life is so sacred that, if someone murders another person, that murderer, who
has assaulted God's image in man, must forfeit his
own life. *Whoever sheds man's blood, by man his
blood shall be shed, for in the image of God he made
man* (Genesis 9:6).

Moreover, because the family is holy in the plan
and sight of God, some of the most severe laws and
punishments in the Bible are aimed at those who
assault the family unit, which is central to God's
holy moral order for human society.

The state has been given the ministry of justice.
Justice demands that the criminal receives the

punishment he deserves. It is as simple as that. The purpose of the death penalty is to administer a penalty that is justly deserved by a criminal in order to make restitution to God's law-order for life. Its purpose is to satisfy God's justice and to vindicate God's law against the defiance of wicked men who try to overturn that law.

The concern of capital punishment is not rehabilitation. It is not even, primarily, deterrence. It is pure justice. Therefore, only God can define capital crimes, and He has clearly done so in the Bible.

## The Power of the Sword in International Affairs

God has given the state the power of the sword in international affairs to protect the citizens of that nation from lawless invaders or terrorists from outside its boundaries. This refers to the national defense of a nation's families.

Why is such a defense needed? The answer is obvious to the Christian. This world we live in is not a perfect one. It is not a sinless utopia, and it will never be so before Jesus Christ returns to earth. There will always be threats to peace and morality to one degree of intensity or another. Therefore, because we live in a fallen world, and because there always will be individuals, movements, institutions, and nations that seek to do harm to the life and property of other people and nations, there will always be the need for the civil government to defend its citizenry with adequate defensive military and strategic capabilities.

For us today in America, there is a more specific reason why God has placed the sword in the hands of the civil government: the global threat of Marxist-Leninist Communism. It is a real threat to those nations with a Christian or even semi-Christian heritage. Why? Why should we consider Marxism-Leninism as a threat to us and to our way of life? Understanding the nature of Marxism will help us understand the answer to that question.

Lenin said that Marxism is Humanism. It is what humanism looks like when it grabs total political and military power. Humanism is the belief that man is God, that man has the ability to determine and define good and evil for himself, with no reference to God and the Bible. Marxism is the political application of humanism, using the strategy of Leninism, which is the use of terrorism to reach one's goals.

A Communist state is one where humanism has absolute control of a society; where Man, represented in the elitist few in power, seeks to predestine and control Man, represented in the masses of men enslaved by the elite, for the purposes of Man, i.e., the elite in control.

What are the basic tenets of Marxism?

**First**, Marxism believes that power determines the course of history. It believes that might makes right; that whoever is in power determines what is right and wrong and then imposes that viewpoint upon the populace. The purpose of Marxism is to use political power to impose its understanding of morality upon the millions of people enslaved by that power.

Communism is a religion that worships power. For Marxism-Leninism sheer, terrifying power controls and determines the course of history. The best illustration of this kind of power religion is seen in Orwell's novel, *1984*, where his character, O'Brian says to Winston,

> We shall squeeze you empty, and then we shall fill you ourselves. Power is in inflicting pain and humiliation. Power is in tearing human minds to pieces and putting them together again in new shapes of your own choosing. Do you begin to see, then what kind of world we are creating? It is the exact opposite of the stupid hedonistic utopias that the old reformers imagined. A world of fear and treachery and torment, a world of trampling and being trampled upon, a world which will grow not less but more merciless as it refines itself.
>
> Progress in our world will be progress toward more pain.... But always — do not forget this, Winston — always there will be the intoxication of power, constantly increasing and constantly growing subtler. Always, at every moment, there be the thrill of victory, the sensation of trampling on the enemy who is helpless. If you want a picture of the future, imagine a boot stamping on a human face — forever.[1]

**Second**, Marxism believes that world politics must be polarized. It must be divided between East and West, between free enterprise and socialism.

---

1. Orwell, George , *1984*, Signet Books, NY, p. 203.

According to Marxism there are two great antagonists in this world — the oppressed and the oppressor, the capitalistic, Christian West and the communistic, non-Christian East.

**Third**, Marxism believes in the principle of "divide and conquer." It is imperialistic in nature. Its goal is the conquest of the world by means of revolution and the destruction of capitalism. It looks for suffering, oppression and dissatisfaction in the world, takes advantage of the situation, polarizes and causes conflict, intensifies the suffering and frustration, in order to create overt revolution and eventual conquest of that nation by militant Communism.

In November, 1987, Gorbachev of the U.S.S.R. said in a speech commemorating the 70th anniversary of the Bolshevik Revolution: "We are moving toward a new world, the world of communism. We shall never turn off that road."

**Fourth**, Marxism believes that there is an irreconcilable war between the Christian system of life and the Marxist system of life. It believes it must, and inevitably will, defeat Christianity. At the base of all their doctrines is the belief that in order for the world to know peace and for all men to be free from oppression, Christianity and its way of life, exhibited in American history, must be rooted out of the earth.

Communism is man's attempt to build a world without God. It has a gospel of dialectics and revolution. It believes that all of history is in conflict: as a certain situation arises in history, THESIS, another opposing situation arises, ANTITHESIS; then, these two come into conflict and a new situation comes into being as a result of this confrontation, SYNTHESIS. The process then begins all over again, ad infinitum.

This makes Marxism revolutionary and violent to the core. All of history is locked into this eternally revolutionary process. Man's only hope for peace and freedom is total revolution. This is the "gospel" of Communism.

The strategy of Communism by which it seeks to reach its goal is obvious. It has been in effect since 1917. It intends to defeat the United States, as the epitome of all it seeks to destroy, because to the Communists the U.S. is the prime example of Christian politics in the world. Its strategy is best summed up by Fred Swartz of the Anti-Communist Crusade: "External encirclement plus internal demoralization plus thermo-nuclear blackmail lead to the progressive surrender of the United States."

The U.S.S.R. and its surrogates are encircling the U.S.A. by hostile powers, viz. Nicaragua and Cuba. They are trying to cut us off from our allies, viz. South Africa. Through subversion by the media and the United Nations, they work to discredit us and demoralize us from within. All the while, they terrorize us at gunpoint with the threat of the biggest build-up of thermo-nuclear power in history. Communism is convinced that this strategy will inevitably bring about the progressive surrender of the U.S.A. to the U.S.S.R.

Perhaps this surrender has already taken place, but it has not been publicized. How can we find out the truth? What does a defeated enemy do for its conqueror? It disarms itself, as we have done in our ABM Treaty, SALT Treaties, INF Treaty, and START Treaty.

It pays tribute to its conqueror. In ancient history, when a people was conquered by an invading army, that people was forced to pay tribute to its victorious invaders. Does the U.S.A. pay tribute to anyone? It sends billions of dollars worth of aid, trade, loans and transfer of technology to communist nations, our avowed enemies. It equips the army of communist Yugoslavia. It sends millions of dollars, in one way or another, to prop up the communist governments of Mozambique, Angola, and Red China. It continually betrays and discredits its allies, such as Taiwan, Nicaragua and South Africa.

Have we already surrendered to the Communists? Consider who ran for president in 1988: the Marxist, Jesse Jackson, who flaunts his Marxism; the radical liberal and socialist, Mike Dukakis; and the pragmatic globalist, former member of the Council of Foreign Relations, and the Tri-lateral Commission (both of which are committed to a one-world government without God), George Bush.

In September, 1990, President Bush, referring to the Iraq situation said, "We now have a New World Order." That incident strengthened the United Nations and brought about the "merger" of the

Soviet Union, the United States, and practically all other governments of the world under the U.N. banner. This has been the goal of the "One World Government" crowd for decades.

Some knowledgeable people think World War III is over and we lost. Phase I was the Cold War of the 1960s. We lost it. Phase II was Detente in the 1970s. We lost it. Phase III, in the 1980s was the encirclement, isolation, terrorization and strangulation of the U.S.A. Phase IV in the 1990s is the progressive surrender of the U.S.A. and its merger with the Soviet system. This requires the gradual abolition of all sovereignty as a nation.

The Thesis—Antithesis—Synthesis principle has been applied. America was changed from a Christian Constitutional Republic into a Democracy then into "Democratic Socialism." We lost much of our individual liberty and our free enterprise system. Russia and its satellites *ostensibly* gave up the harsh and bloody reign of terror in favor of "Democratic Socialism." So the Thesis (Liberty) was challenged by the Antithesis (Communism) and the result is Synthesis (Democratic Socialism).

Whenever atheistic, totalitarian Communism establishes itself, it murders people by the thousands and millions. Since the Bolshevik Revolution in 1917, over 200 million people have died as a result of Communism. For the phoniness of Gorbachev's "Glasnost" and "Perestroika" see *New Lies For Old* by Anatolly Golitzsyn and "Gorbachev's Challenge: Detente II," the report of the task force on the dangers of Detente II.

It should be obvious why God has given the state the power of the sword in international relationships. The state must be the defender and shield which stands between hostile, aggressive, lawless forces (like Communism) and the law-abiding families within a nation (Proverbs 24:11,12).

Nothing else, on a human level, stands between us and a hostile world except the defensive power of a godly nation. A people is secure from those invaders and terrorists who would destroy their Christian way of life only when the federal government of that nation realizes and implements its God-given responsibility to use that sword to protect them from those enemies.

The Bible teaches that a strong defense of a nation deters aggression and helps preserve the peace — peace through superior strength — militarily, strategically and spiritually. The stronger a nation is spiritually and militarily, the more secure that godly nation will be.

This is also the teaching of the New Testament (Luke 11:21; Luke 14:31). In Luke 11 we find Jesus making the point that He will win the victory over Satan, and that His ability to cast out demons is proof of that fact. He uses a military analogy, which was a commonly understood principle of His day — superior military strength deters aggression against a nation.

He said:

> When a strong man, fully armed, guards his own

homestead, his possessions are undisturbed; but
when someone stronger than he attacks him and
overpowers him, he takes away from him all his armor
on which he had relied, and distributes his plunder
(Luke 11:21-22).

Jesus is not primarily concerned with military
defense, but He is using an analogy which He
considers a correct one. In order for a strong man to
protect what he owns, he must have superior power
to anyone who would rob him or do him harm. If he
does not have superior strength, he will not be able
to protect that for which he is responsible.

In Luke 14:31-32 we read:

Or what king, when he sets out to meet another
king in battle, will not first sit down and take counsel
whether he is strong enough with ten thousand men to
encounter the one coming against him with twenty
thousand? Or else, while the other is still far away, he
sends a delegation and asks for terms of peace.

If an army is on the verge of invading a nation,
that nation had better have a stronger defense than
the offensive power of the invader, or else that
nation had better begin peace negotiations immedi-
ately.

Another perspective than the one Jesus held has
dominated American foreign policy for over forty
years, called by its proponents, Mutual Assured
Destruction. This policy is built upon a principle of
retaliation rather than one of actual defense of the
citizenry. It has rendered the United States defenseless against missile attack. It maintains the
peace by making the American people totally vul-

nerable to a nuclear first strike against the United States.

If a hostile power should launch a missile attack killing millions of American people, we will retaliate, killing millions of the enemy's civilians in return. This is immoral. Because of our policy of peace through weakness and disarmament, the United States is continually and increasingly intimidated and terrorized by the USSR and her surrogates.

At this point in time, we have no means whatsoever to defend ourselves from nuclear attack, as a result of the deliberate policy of both Republican and Democratic administrations. If any power were to launch a missile against us, all we could do is absorb the death of millions, and then decide whether to retaliate, kill millions of their men, women and children, or surrender.

This foreign policy is in direct disobedience to the Word of God. It neglects or denies the power and responsibility God has given the state to protect us. It is a foreign policy which is not only immoral, it has the potential of being murderous to our families. God has given the state the power of the sword to protect families from those who would harm or destroy them.

However, we must never lose sight of the fact that, ultimately, the security and strength of the nation is not in its chariots and nuclear might. We need chariots. We need a defense program that actually defends us, such as the Strategic Defense

Initiative (High Frontier). We need a Peace Shield, a non-nuclear, space-based defense system capable of protecting us from missiles launched against us, which would make nuclear weaponry obsolete.

But, in the final analysis, we must not put our faith in missiles, or SDI, or conventional military power, or arms treaties. Our ultimate and final security is Almighty God, our ultimate Peace Shield (Psalm 3:3f), if we, as a nation, are being faithful to Him.

This in no way implies that we may sit back and say, "Well, we are going to trust God, so we are for nuclear disarmament and nuclear freeze." A person who says this is like that person who stands on the railroad tracks and says, "I am going to trust God to take care of me while I sit on these tracks. He will keep the train from hitting me."

The Bible, however, teaches us that we are responsible to God for our actions as individuals and nations. We are accountable to obey the Bible as we trust in God. We must "trust in God and keep our powder dry," as Oliver Cromwell told his troops.

It is the God-given responsibility of the state to trust in God alone and to be adequately prepared to protect its citizens from criminals, terrorists and invaders. It is immoral to do otherwise.

But, having said that, we must clearly understand that a nation with the best defense shield and superior conventional and strategic capabilities, but which has left God, is insecure and will fall. If, on the other hand, a nation is doing its best to protect itself, but its defense capabilities are relatively low, but it is faithful to God, no superior power on earth can harm one hair on the head of any of its citizens without the will of our Father who is in heaven.

Rand has well-written:

> The greatest army in the world with the finest equipment, backed by an aerial force surpassing in striking power and numbers, any combination that could be sent into the air against it, with an impregnable navy, including all necessary auxiliaries and transport, all this might, backed by the military genius of a leadership which could not be matched or excelled in military tactics, would still be powerless to overcome his people if they had set their own house in order. For when Israel was in a proper spiritual relationship to God, enabling their spiritual leaders to declare with authority, "Neither be terrified, for the Lord your God, it is He that goes with you, to fight for you against your enemies to save you," no combination of military might upon the face of this earth can defeat them, (*Digest of the Divine Law*, Destiny Publishers).

This must be our faith (Deuteronomy 20). We must not put our faith in bombs or bullets. We call upon our federal government to be faithful to the task God Himself has given to it, and use the power of the sword to protect us from international terrorists. A nation that sheaths that sword because of partiality, that surfeits it in lawless cruelty, that retires it because of humanistic sentimentality, that denies its right of existence, or that wields it beyond its limited domain stands condemned by Almighty God.

We recognize that, even if we were superior militarily to the U.S.S.R. — which in 1991 we are not — without a deep and genuine return to God in Christ as our Lord and Savior, and to God's Word as the source of our law and salvation, our military superiority would not be sufficient to protect us from whatever instrument God used to bring judgment on us, as He used the Babylonians to judge Israel for her rebellion. **Without national repentance, all our might will not protect us.**

The Bible makes clear the legitimacy of just and defensive wars, when necessary, to protect a citizenry when that is the only remaining alternative to preserve a Christian moral order, after diplomacy has failed. As horrible as it is, in this fallen world, sometimes war is the only way left open to us to thwart and restrain lawless man's revolt against God and man.

There are things worse than war: one is slavery, another is the death of the family. In fact, the Bible goes so far as to say that it is sinful to refuse to fight for the protection of your people in a just war. Numbers 32:20-23 says that your sins will find you out if you refuse to fight in a just war:

> So Moses said to them, "If you will do this, if you will arm yourselves before the Lord for the war, and all of your armed men cross over the Jordan before the Lord until He has driven His enemies out from before Him, and the land is subdued before the Lord, then afterward you shall return and be free of obligation toward the Lord and toward Israel, and this land shall be yours for a possession before the Lord. But if you will not do so, behold, you have sinned against the Lord,

and be sure your sin will find you out."

Not only is such refusal to fight sinful, but, on the other hand, if the federal government calls upon us to fight in an unjust war, it would be sinful to do anything else than to conscientiously object. A Christian may not fight in an unjust war. Why? Because the Bible says, *thou shalt not commit murder.*

Many people object to this view of national "self-defense" and just wars. Some would say, "Doesn't the Bible condemn killing in the Ten Commandments?" The Sixth Commandment literally reads: *Thou shalt not commit murder* (Exodus 20:13).

Later in Exodus 21:12, God through Moses says that the civil government is to put to death anybody that commits murder. Therefore, the Sixth Commandment must not be interpreted as prohibiting every form of legal killing, such as capital punishment. Capital punishment, as we have seen, is taught in the Bible as essential to the maintenance of a godly order. Self-defense and just, defensive wars are also condoned in the Bible. But the Bible clearly prohibits the murdering of innocent people without valid and legal cause, viz. abortion.

Others object by saying that this view of the power of the sword is contrary to Jesus' teaching on love. They say, "Should not love and forgiveness dominate life? Did not Jesus say to love our enemies?" But that is not the only thing Jesus said or did. In John 2:13-16, Jesus used violent and potentially deadly force to clean out the Temple of thieves and frauds. It was His prerogative to do so as the Head of the Church and Ruler of the kings of the earth (Revelation 1:5).

In John 2:15 we read, *and He* (Jesus) *made a scourge of cords....* This was not a feather duster. A "scourge of cords" is several leather straps with sharp and heavy pieces of bone and metal in the end of each leather strap. When it struck a person, it would not only rip and tear out flesh, it could very easily kill, blind, maim, or fracture bones.

So, in John 2:14-16 we read,

> And He found in the temple those who were selling oxen and sheep and doves, and money-changers seated. And He made a scourge of cords, and drove them all out of the temple, with the sheep and the oxen; and He poured out the coins of the money-changers, and overturned their tables; and to those who were selling the doves He said, "Take these things away; stop making my Father's house a house of merchandise."

Imagine the picture. Tables overturned! People probably jumping out of windows and running out of doors to escape Jesus swinging His scourge of cords. This was the use of violent force to maintain God's moral order. It was not inconsistent with anything else Jesus ever said, since as the Son of God, everything He did was thoroughly righteous and everything He spoke was thoroughly infallible.

In Luke 22 we find Jesus sending out His apostles into the world. He knows He is about to leave them, so He sends them out into a hostile world to preach the gospel. He knows it will be a dangerous world for them. So, he tells them to acquire sidearms, i.e., swords. In Luke 22:35-36 He says,

> "When I sent you out without purse and bag and sandals, you did not lack anything, did you?" And they said, "No, nothing." And He said to them, "But now, let him who has a purse take it along, likewise also a bag, and let him who has no sword sell his robe and buy one."

There is nothing contrary to the Ten Commandments or to Jesus' teaching on love in the just and godly use of the sword by the state for the maintenance of God's moral order and the protection of law-abiding people. In fact, if the state does not use the sword to enforce biblical law, God will see to it that the sword will be used against that state in judgment.

We must remember that Jehovah, the Lord of Israel and of all the world's nations, is at war with His enemies. He has said that He will not rest in His war against the Amalekites (Old Testament terrorists), until their very memory is blotted out from the face of the earth (Deuteronomy 25:17-19).

Remember that Jesus Christ is at war with those who persist in their rebellion against God's order. In Revelation 19 He is pictured as riding on a great stallion with the blood of His enemies splattered all over His clothes, having just defeated them.

We must also remember that it was Jesus who said, *I did not come to bring peace; but a sword* (Matthew 10:34). The greatest example of His war against those who oppose Him was His death on the cross and His resurrection from the grave by which

He did battle with Satan and defeated him (Hebrews 2:14).

Throughout history, through Providence and through the faithfulness of Christians applying God's Word to every area of life, Jesus Christ continues to wage war against His enemies until all His enemies are put down in every area of life (I Corinthians 15:25f).

We must work harder in praying and in calling for the restoration of a strong defense of American citizens by our federal government; for the restoration of the just use of the sword in the protection of our lives, families, property and freedoms; in the maintenance of order and peace; in the enforcement of biblical law; in the punishment of criminals, terrorists and invaders; and in the reshaping of our foreign policy with reference to Communism on solidly biblical principles. If we as a nation do not return to these biblical principles and duties, the sword will be used against us (Isaiah 10:5-6).

# CHAPTER FIVE

# *The Power to Tax*

*For because of this you also pay taxes, for rulers are servants of God, devoting themselves to this very thing* (Romans 13:6). God has given the state the power to tax, along with the power to administer God's law, and the power of the sword. He has given it the power to tax for the specific purpose of enabling the state to enforce biblical law and to protect its people. Therefore, taxes, when biblical, must not be viewed as tyrannical.

According to Romans 13:6, there is such a thing as a just tax, when it is used in order to allow the state to carry out its duties as the servant of God and the minister of justice to terrorize the lawless and to avenge the wrath of God upon evil behavior. It takes money to provide adequately for a police force, a military force, and a judicial system.

### The Presupposition of Taxation

The Bible teaches us that the power to tax presupposes the claim of ownership and sovereignty. The power to tax is the claim of control and ownership over man and his possessions, or whatever is taxed. For instance, when a civil government unjustly claims the right to deprive a man of his liberty and property because he refuses to pay taxes, that state is claiming to own that man and to have ultimate sovereignty over him and his property.

When a state creates a system of unjust taxes upon the populace, it is presupposing that it owns that populace and its property. Taxation presupposes sovereignty and the right of control. If you think that is an exaggeration, try not paying your property taxes and see who gets your home.

The presupposition of income tax, property tax and inheritance tax is that the state owns your income, your property, your family's future, and everything about you.

What is a tax? It is a state-imposed levy by which your wealth is forcibly taken from you for the state's use. All non-biblical taxes presuppose that the state owns you and has the right of control over you. The assumption is that the state can confiscate your property for whatever reason it sees fit.

But, of course, since man is Jehovah's creature, Jehovah's subject, and the steward of Jehovah's creation, no one else may be his Lord; hence, no one and no human institution, including the state, has the right to tax anybody beyond what God has commanded.

There is only one absolute proprietor and sovereign in the universe — Almighty God. Therefore, only He has absolute ownership and control over all men and all of man's institutions. Only Jehovah has the right to govern and regulate your life and property. Only Jehovah owns you. Only Jehovah is Sovereign.

Neither individuals nor states have sovereignty before Him. He is the Lord. The fullness of the earth and all it contains belong to Him alone. All authority in heaven and on earth belong to Him and to His Son, Jesus Christ. *The earth is the Lord's and the fulness thereof, the world and they that dwell therein, for He hath founded it upon the seas and established it upon the floods* (Psalm 24:1).

What does all this imply? *Only Jehovah can impose taxes!* When any man or human institution imposes taxes not originating with the law of God, that man or institution is denying God's ownership of His creation, and is seeking to establish his/its own autonomy apart from God and his/its sovereignty over man.

All such attempts must be viewed as rebellion against Almighty God, the Sovereign of the universe. Professed Christians who refuse to oppose such claims by man and the state may bear the mark of the Beast and could be classified as accomplices to thieves trying to play God.

When the civil government claims to be God by unjust taxation, it must be opposed by the people of God. It is an act of idolatry to bow before a human institution recognizing as valid its claim of lordship and ownership over your life. *You shall have no other gods before me,* said Jehovah, the one true God.

Humanistic taxation is idolatrous. It claims lordship over your person, income, property and future. It is a direct attempt to rob God of His lordship of creation. It is a denial of the fact that all property and life in America belong to Jehovah. In recognition of this biblical principle, the U. S. Constitution does not allow for the ownership of land by the federal government, except for that which is necessary for military installations and government buildings. Yet, at present, the federal government owns more land in America than there is land east of the Mississippi River.

American government is playing God by claiming ownership of and sovereignty over American land and people. The U. S. Constitution also did not allow for the levying of income taxes by the federal government. The IRS is a clear indictment against America for her rebellion against God.

In I Samuel 8:9f we find that Israel was tired of having God rule over her. She wanted a human king like her neighboring nations. She was embarrassed before the world that God was her ruler. So, she rejected God's rule for the rule of man.

She became a humanistic state, where man, not Jehovah, is judge, lawgiver and king. In verses 9-15 God warned Israel about what would happen when she changed gods:

> "Now then, listen to their voice; however, you shall solemnly warn them and tell them of the procedure of the king who will reign over them." So Samuel spoke all the words of the Lord to the people who had asked of him a king. And he said, "This will be the procedure of the king who will reign over you: he will take your sons and place them for himself in his chariots and among his horsemen and they will run before his chariots. And he will appoint for himself commanders of thousands and of fifties, and some to do his plowing and to reap his harvest and to make his weapons of war and equipment for his chariots. He will also take your daughters for perfumers and cooks and bakers. And he will take the best of your fields and your vineyards and your olive groves, and give them to his

servants. And he will take a tenth of your seed and of your vineyards, and give to his officers and to his servants."

This is what happens to a nation whenever it turns from God to man, as its source of law: the massive growth of a choking bureaucracy regulating everything, the socialization of agriculture and industry, the drafting of men and women in unjust political wars, and the establishment of an oppressive taxation system that will steal from its citizens one-tenth or more of their incomes.

That was one of the signs that Israel had rejected God and that God was judging Israel: the state taxed them one-tenth of their income. In other words, when the state taxes you a tenth of your income, or more, God views that state as trying to play God, because God requires only a tenth. In the United States in 1991 the total amount of taxes the average working man pays in city, county, state, federal, sales taxes, and others, is the entirety of his income from January to June each year. That spells involuntary servitude, i.e., slavery to the state half of our lives every year. Do you enjoy being a slave of the state? What are you going to do about it?

## The Nature of Taxation

Because humanistic taxation is idolatrous, imitating the true God, it strives to be all-encompassing. It tries to cover all the specifics of life, closing all "loop-holes." In some states caramel-covered popcorn is taxed, while buttered popcorn is not. In other states ice cubes in alcoholic beverages are taxed, while ice cubes in a soft drink are not. We will continue to see more and more taxation on the specifics and details of life because the goal of the state that thinks it is God is total control and total taxation, because it believes it possesses total ownership and total sovereignty.

During the "conservative" administrations of Ronald Reagan and George Bush, Americans experienced the largest tax increases ever imposed on them. Expect to pay more taxes in the future. Why? Because in a nation that believes it is God, the only way it can obtain total control over all of us is to impose total taxation, which is consistent with the nation's underlying faith that the state owns everything and everybody.

So, it becomes obvious that humanistic taxation is not only idolatrous and all-encompassing, like an octopus, it is also destructive and decapitalizing to man.

R. J. Rushdoony and Edward Powell have written an excellent book entitled *Tithing and Dominion* on the subject of taxation.[1] It is astute in its insights as the following quotation shows:

> This destructive principle of ungodly state taxation can be seen in every area of life. Businesses, and charitable foundations, etc., are licensed (a pagan form of taxation), which means that they operate at

---

1. Rushdoony, R. J., and Powell, E. A., *Tithing And Dominion,* (Ross House Books, 1979, Vallecito, CA.), p. 57. My comments on taxation are greatly influenced by this book.

the pleasure of the state, and are, thus, owned by the state.

Doctors, dentists, teachers, mechanics, plumbers, etc., are also licensed by the state (a pagan form of taxation), except that in these latter cases, the state claims ownership of a man through its claim of ownership of his profession and trade. Inheritance is taxed to demonstrate that the family is owned by the state.

Since the state never wants any one family, or group of families, to become too powerful (unless they are part of the state elite), its taxation on inheritance is oppressive and destructive. The state taxes property, and thus claims ownership of a man's home. The "owner" merely rents his home from the state.

Property taxes especially decapitalize the elderly, and poorer members of society, because their incomes seldom keep up with the rising tax burden. Sales taxes decapitalize the lower and middle income members of society since they must spend a larger portion of their incomes than the upper income groups. The state taxes electricity, clothing, food, drugs, tires, etc.

There is hardly any area of life that the state does not claim ownership of by its power to tax. The list of items taxed is only limited by the imagination and energy of the state bureaucracy.

The humanistic tax system decapitalizes man all across the board and is destructive in every area of life — society, morality, and the economy.

Consider the Income Tax: It is based on the Marxist principle that the responsibility of the state is to forcibly take the wealth of the producers and to redistribute it to people in need, when, in fact, most of it stays in the hands of federal and state bureaucrats. It punishes successful, hard-working men and women. It is regressive and oppressive and unfair. It lessens production, causes unemployment, raises prices and costs, decreases earnings, and breeds envy.

Consider Corporation Taxes: The current practice is to tax large profit-making corporations. But corporations do not pay taxes; only *people* pay taxes. When a corporation is taxed, the money for the new tax is secured through higher prices, lower wages, and less production.

Consider Property Taxes: It is a direct assault upon the family as well as an assault on the sovereign ownership of all land by God. Neither the state government, nor the federal government has the right to tax the property of its citizens, because, in reality, the civil government has no property to tax. *The earth is the Lord's, and all it contains* (Psalm 24:1). *He owns the cattle on a thousand hills* (Psalm 50:10). When the state taxes your property, it is taking off its mask and revealing that it assumes it is God.

Consider the Inheritance Tax: It is a clear assault on the family and its future. It destroys a family's future; and it is expressly forbidden in Ezekiel 46:18.

Withholding Taxes are also forbidden. The Bible teaches that the firstfruits of our labors belong to the Lord, not to the state. In the Old Testament that which was taken off the top of the people's incomes, was not a withholding tax, it was the offering of firstfruits to the Lord, symbolizing that all they possessed and produced belonged to Jehovah, not to the state. Withholding earnings before a person can tithe puts God in second place behind the state.

Hidden taxes, such as a Value-added Tax, are deceitful and companions of fraud and injustice. Social Security Taxes on the Churches and on individuals are also destructive. Social Security taxes on individuals have increased over 650% since the program began, and it has increased unemployment significantly. It has lessened Americans' ability to save. It has caused 97% of everybody over 65 years of age to be utterly dependent upon a humanistic state for their very existence. It also defrauds and robs young adults who will never see any of their money in return from a Social Security program that is well on its way to bankruptcy before the turn of the century. (It is already bankrupt, however, nobody will admit it.)

The most destructive, most vicious and best hidden of all humanistic taxes is Inflation, the increase of the money supply by the state and the Federal Reserve (a private corporation which controls the money of America). It decapitalizes all of society because it destroys the currency upon which that society makes its economic decisions and judgments.

As a currency goes, so goes the nation. We must be clear on this: inflation is not caused by higher salaries and increasing prices, as we are led to believe. Inflation is the increase of the money supply by the state, generating paper money, expanding credit, and monetizing debts by fiat.

Inflation is the increase of money, unbacked by gold and silver. As the money supply is increased, the value of the dollar is decreased and prices begin to rise. But, while that is true, we must also understand that the state tries to be God by inflation and the control of money, because the citizens have "larceny in their hearts," i.e., the love of money, which is the root of all evil.

Isaiah 1 says that one of the reasons God punished Israel was that political leaders inflated her money supply, thereby creating a dishonest economy that devastated those on fixed incomes, viz. widows, and which cheapened production. Israel's leaders created a corrupted currency because Israel's people were already corrupted. God had to come and burn the dross out of that culture in order to restore it. For an insightful book on inflation, see R. J. Rushdoony's The Roots *of Inflation* (Ross House Books, 1982, Vallecito, CA).

## The Biblical System of Taxation

The power to tax is the power to bless or to destroy. Taxation can be a blessing, when it is used to provide funds to enable the state to be the minister of God's justice; or it can be a curse when it is used for any other purpose.

That which determines whether a system of taxation will be a blessing or a curse is the moral base upon which it is constructed. Whom does the state, which imposes the tax, recognize as the ultimate sovereign and owner of man and creation? Itself or

Jehovah?

The biblical system of taxation is built on the sovereignty and ownership of the God revealed in the Bible, who is the Creator of the universe. Therefore, it is a blessing to the nation which practices it.

God taxes everything *in principle*. He does not tax everything specifically. Therefore, biblical taxation is not destructive nor decapitalizing. God taxes everything in principle with *three basic taxes* revealed in the Bible.

First, is the Tax of the Sabbath. The Sabbath is a tax on our time and energy. God says we owe Him one day in seven to worship Him and to rest from six days of carrying out our callings under His rule and blessing.

Second, is the Tax of the Tithe. This is God's tax on our possessions, productivity, and earnings. He commands us to give Him 10% of what we earn in order to finance the advance of the kingdom of God and the carrying out of the Great Commission. This is God's tax on our use of His land.

The third is the Head Tax of Exodus 30:11-16. This is the only tax in the Bible which the state may levy on its citizens. It is a flat-rate tax: everybody paid the same low amount. The individual citizens of Israel were taxed 110 grains of silver annually to maintain the civil government as God's minister of justice.

Tithes and offerings, not the head tax, were used to provide for the health, education and welfare of the citizens of Israel. Note also that the tithe was not paid to the civil government.

The head tax was a flat rate charged regardless of one's earnings. It was an equal amount charged to all of the citizens. There was no income tax, no property tax, no inheritance tax, no hidden taxes, no sales tax, no Social Security tax, no inflation tax. Everybody was charged the same amount, and that took care of maintaining the judicial system, the police force and the military.

Why does God benignly impose these three taxes: Sabbath, tithe, and head tax? These are the practical ways by which God declares His ownership and sovereignty over us. It is as if He said: "Give me one day out of seven to show that you believe that I own every second of your time. Give me a tenth of your income to show me that you believe that I own everything you are and everything you have. Give the state the required head tax, so they can administer my rule and enforce my law."

This is why refusal to pay God any one of His divinely revealed taxes is rebellion against Him. If we refuse to keep the Sabbath or to tithe or to pay the head tax, we are saying that we do not believe God is sovereign. And if the state administers any other tax but the one God has required, the state is saying that God is not sovereign. And if we defend the state's pretended right to levy unbiblical taxes, without criticizing it for doing so, we are saying that we believe the state is sovereign.

# The Reconstruction of America's Tax System

How can we reform our unjust, humanistic tax system in the United States of America? How can we abolish the IRS? Unless our tax system is radically and biblically reformed, it will lead to the total control of an all-inclusive state, which thinks it is God, and which will destroy our economy.

America's tax system cannot be brought down by violence or revolution. There were zealots, or for-mer-revolutionaries, among Jesus' own disciples. They realized that Rome was totalitarian in its authority. They thought it had to be brought down in order for people to be free. But instead of working by God's method in the Bible, i.e., the Christian reconstruction of every area of life and thought by the Word of God, they wanted to do it by violent, immediate revolution.

The situation is described in Matthew 22:15-17:

> Then the Pharisees went and counseled together how they might trap Him in what He said. And they sent their disciples to Him, along with the Herodians, saying, 'Teacher, we know that you are truthful and teach the way of God in truth, and defer to no one; for you are not partial to any. Tell us therefore, what do you think? Is it lawful to give a poll-tax to Caesar, or not?"

These revolutionaries were advising people not to pay taxes of any kind to Caesar, because he was an anti-Christian dictator and his poll-tax was not required in the Bible. They were saying that to pay that tax is to compromise God.

In reality, however, these men were hypocrites seeking only to get out of paying taxes and to embarrass Jesus. Jesus' response was forthright in Matthew 22:18-21:

> But Jesus perceived their malice, and said, "Why are you testing me, you hypocrites? Show me the coin used for the poll-tax." And they brought Him a denarius. And He said to them, "Whose likeness and inscription is this?" They said to Him, "Caesar's." Then He said to them, "Then render to Caesar the things that are Caesar's; and to God the things that are God's."

What does it mean to give to God the things that belong to God? What belongs to God? *Everything!* So the principle here is: Render to God what is His due, i.e., everything. We are called upon here by Jesus to give God everything and absolute, unqualified loyalty in everything we do.

Now the basis of Jesus' argument is this: Because Caesar's image is on the coin in question, it belongs to Caesar. And because Caesar bears the image of God, his Creator, Caesar belongs to God. As the Emperor of Rome, Caesar is to give God what is His due: everything Caesar is and has. Heads of state, bearing God's image, are to give God what is His due: obedience to His revealed will, recognition of His supremacy, and undivided allegiance to His authority.

Jesus tells His questioners, in so many words: "Give Caesar what is due him. It is his coin. His reign is oppressive and unrighteous. His administration and taxes are all unbiblical. He must be stopped. His kingdom must be altered and Christianized. But it must be done my way, not your way. Revolution will not accomplish my goals. If you do not pay this tax, Caesar's soldiers will put you in jail, and then you will be of no help to anybody, only a burden on your family. So pay the tax."

Allegiance to Christ takes precedence over all other allegiances. Therefore, this counsel from Jesus concerning the denarius is relevant. Humanistic taxes are to be paid, unless paying them prohibits us from obeying Jesus.

So, how can we bring down our present tax system?

*First,* replace every political leader who votes like he believes that the state has original ownership and sovereignty over our lives, incomes, property and future. That kind of leader is better suited for the USSR than for the USA.

*Second,* begin to obey God's tax system yourself with the Sabbath and the tithe. Give Him His tax on your time and on your use of His land. Whatever you must give up, whatever you must readjust, whatever you must change, give God His due. Spend Sundays in rest and worship with your family and Christian friends. Give the Lord 10% of your income.

*Third,* the only way to abolish the IRS and reconstruct the tax system of the U.S. is through evangelism. There is no other way to do it. Tax revolt will not do it. Our current politicians won't do it. Current voters won't do it.

In a culture that believes the state has the right

of ownership, sovereignty and control over us, the only thing that will get us back to God's head-tax, and no other civil taxes, is for us, as the Church of Jesus Christ, and as Christian citizens, in the power of God, to persuade men and women to believe that all ownership and authority belongs to Jesus Christ (Matthew 28:18), not to man or the state.

Until American citizens quit looking to the state to be his/her lord and savior, until he/she stands in opposition to that view, there will be no change in the present tax system or in the current suicidal direction of our civil government. It will become increasingly burdensome and oppressive.

Writing letters to congressmen and senators is important, but it is not enough. Complaining about the IRS is not enough. Unless we are working personally week in and week out "begging" (II Corinthians 5) people to become real Christians, to believe that Jesus Christ possesses all ownership, sovereignty, and salvation which is received by grace through faith, we can expect no relief.

Jesus Christ is the Lord and Savior of the world. It is that truth that will abolish the Internal Revenue Service, when Americans start believing it again.

CHAPTER SIX

# *The Counterproductivity of not Linking Christianity and Politics*

## A Reply to Senator Mark Hatfield

Published in
*The Theology of Christian Resistance*
A Symposium edited by Dr. Gary North
Geneva Divinity School Press, Tyler, Texas
(1983)

"Before Christians today can hope to make any contribution to the solution of the social and political ills afflicting our nation this is an imperative: they must dispose of the humanist myth of the neutrality of politics so far as religion is concerned."[1]

What is religious neutrality in politics? Hebden Taylor answers, "According to this neutrality principle Christians may participate in the political process only as citizens but never as believers. Thus in his book *The Christian in Politics* Walter James argues:

> The Christian is called upon to act beside other men and no assurance is given him that he will sense God's purpose better than they. He can no more aim to be a Christian statesman than a Christian engineer. Politics has at any one time its own techniques, aims and standards, vary though they may, and in the light of them as they are in his lifetime, the Christian's effort must be to make a good politician and no more.
>
> He stands on a par with the non-Christian, just as there are no denominations in the science of physics. His religion will give him no special guidance in his public task, as it will do within his personal relationships with close neighbors.

In thus advocating that Christians must abide by the prevailing doctrine of neutrality which seeks to exclude religion from politics and in suggesting that Christians should restrict their religion to the field

---

1. Taylor, E. L Hebden., *The Myth of Religious Neutrality in Politics*, p. 1, unpub.

of personal relationships, James has neatly fallen right into the secular liberal humanist trap which tries to place religion alongside man's other activities and interests, whether these be academic, social, economic, political, or artistic.

This modern idea of religion is one which the secular apostate world around us today loves to have Christians accept. Secular humanists have no objection to our Christian faith at all, provided we reserve it strictly for ourselves in the privacy of our homes and church buildings, and just so long as we do not try to live up to our Christian principles in our business and public life.

> On no account must the Spirit and Word of the Lord Jesus Christ be allowed to enter the ballot booth or the market place where the real decisions of modern life are made, nor must religion interfere with such vital matters as education, politics, labor relations, profits and wages. These activities are all supposed to be 'neutral' and they can therefore be withdrawn from sectarian influences so that the secular spirit of the community may prevail. This is the spirit of reason, science and pure technique of the practical pragmatist. For him truth is only what works out in practice and for whom the God of the Bible is thought to be the projection of the father image or at least a being concocted out of man's image of himself or of the society in which he lives.[2]

Bernard Zylstra has well spoken in *Challenge and Response*,

> Neutralism is the view that man can live wholly or

---

2. Ibid. p. 1

partly without taking God's Word into account. Those
who pay homage to the fiction of neutrality maintain
that many segments of modern culture are merely
technical. It is then thought that a corporation, a
union, a school, a government can be run by making
exclusively factual, technical decisions which have no
relation to one's ultimate perspective on the basic
issues.... This "technalism" is the result of a pragmatic philosophy. The defenders of "technalism" are
among the most dangerous guides to a wholly secular
world. For it is inevitable that the realm of the "neutral" and the "factual" will constantly increase until it
has swallowed all of human morality and faith.[3]

Religious neutrality in politics has been advo-
cated in a recent *Congressional Record* (Volume
126, Number 66) by Senator Mark Hatfield, who es-
pouses "evangelical" Christianity. The title of this
article (p. S4271) reveals its main thrust, "The
Counterproductive Linking of Religion and Politics." In this speech, which is a response to the
Washington for Jesus Rally on April 29, 1980,
Senator Hatfield commends the leadership of that
rally for not "linking their religious concerns with
so-called political issues." He says "I want to commend them for seeing the danger in such a strategy
and putting aside an organized lobbying effort on
issues which people of goodwill have a difference of
opinion." Bear in mind that those attending the
rally were fellow "evangelical" Christians.

Senator Hatfield included in his speech an article
by Stanley Mooneyham, entitled, "United We Fall."

---

3. Zylstra, Bernard, *Challenge and Response*, p. 2

In this article, Mooneyham misinterprets and mis-applies several biblical texts to make his point:

> I am as scared of an evangelical power bloc as I am of any other.... Although it is not impossible to harmo-nize the two in some situations, there is actually a basic conflict between Christian commitment and political power. The strength of faith is in its ava-lanche of powerlessness, its tidal force of love. If politics is the art of achieving the possible, faith is the art of achieving the impossible. Politics says, "Destroy your enemies." Christian faith says, "Love your ene-mies." Politics says, "The end justifies the means." Christian faith says, "The means validates the end." Politics says, "The first shall be first." Christian faith says, "The last shall be first."

Mooneyham's redefining of faith and dichotomyz-ing of faith and politics is tantamount to making faith irrational, contentless and irrelevant and to making politics autonomous, pragmatic, and sover-eign. It sounds like he found his definition in Karl Marx or some other advocate of secular pragma-tism. Furthermore, man-as-individual or man-in-society is dependent upon Almighty God, Who alone is autonomous and sovereign — so believes the Christian.

Senator Hatfield refers to a second article written by Charles Bergstrom entitled, "When the Self-Righteous Rule, Watch Out!" This article is an attack on evangelicals who believe the Bible is to be used as a political textbook, as our founding fathers believed. Mr. Bergstrom sets up a man of straw and then proceeds to knock him down. His exaggeration of the position he is opposing shows that he does not really understand that position.

He identifies those Christians who "read the Bible without a sense of mystery and ambiguity" with those who gave us "the Crusades, the Spanish Inquisition and the Salem witchcraft trials." He goes on to intimate that these Christians are self-righteous, because they hold this position. I thought only God could see the heart?!

There are two fundamental weaknesses with this position held by Senator Hatfield concerning religious neutrality in the political arena. First, there is a misunderstanding of the relationship of religion to culture (life, including politics). And, second, there is an (unintentional) denial of two basic principles of Christianity: (1) the Lordship of Jesus Christ over all of life; and (2) the all-embracing authority of the law of God.

What is the relationship of religion to culture (life), according to the teachings of the Bible, and recognized by many Christians and non-Christians alike? This is not an irrelevant theological debate. It is central to the whole discussion of the role of the Christian and of Christianity in American politics. A misunderstanding here can be, and has been, devastating for Americans.

What do we mean by the word, religion? It is "the binding tendency in every man to dedicate himself with his whole heart to the true God or an idol,"[4]

---

4. Lee, F. N., *The Central Significance of Culture*, Presbyterian and Reformed Publishing Co., Nutley, N. J., 1976, p. 121

according to F. Nigel Lee. In this sense all men are religious because no man can escape being a man in the image of God created to worship and serve God, rebellious and unregenerate though he be. Romans 1:25 says, *For they* (mankind) *exchanged the truth of God for a lie, and worshipped and served the creature rather than the Creator ...* Man is inescapably religious.

What do we mean by the word, culture? It is religion externalized. Culture "is the unavoidable result of man's necessary efforts to use and to develop the world in which he lives either under the guidance of the Lord or under the influence of sin, in accordance with whichever of the two controls his heart. As such, culture includes all of man's works — arts, science, agriculture, literature, language, astronomical investigations, rites of worship, domestic life, social customs (his politics) — in short, the cultural products of the whole of man's life stand either in the service of God or in the service of an idol," writes Lee.[5] Man was created by God for culture, i.e., to "cult-ivate" the garden (Genesis 2:15); to multiply and have dominion over the earth (Genesis 1:28). He cannot escape his calling, although unregenerate man perverts it, while regenerate man does it for the glory of God and in submission to God's command.

Now concerning the relationship of religion to culture. It bears a similar relationship as faith does

---

5. Ibid. p. 123

to works. Works grow from the root of faith and are expressions of that faith. *Faith without works is dead,* according to James 2:26. Culture is religion externalized. It is the outgrowth and expression of the religion of the people.

All cultures, then, are thoroughly religious and never can be a-religious. (That is not to say that they are all theistic. For instance, humanism, as recognized by the U. S. Supreme Court [Torcaso vs. Watson], is a non-theistic religion, believing only in man.)

Every aspect of a nation's life will reflect, and cannot help but reflect, the religion of the citizenry, whatever that religion may be. Religious neutrality in politics, and in every other facet of a nation's culture and life, is a myth. Because religion (faith) is all-inclusive, all human activity will be colored by the religion (faith) one holds. There are no neutral cultural activities, as there are no neutral "works"; they are either "good works" or "evil deeds," done either to the glory of the God of the Bible or to the glory of an idol (non-god). Van Til writes on this subject, that:

> Culture is not something neutral, without ethical or religious connotation. Human achievement is not purposeless but seeks to achieve certain ends, which are either good or bad. (For the Christian, the one standard of morality, public and private, is the Bible.) Since man is a moral being, his culture cannot be a-moral.
>
> Because man is a religious being, his culture, too, must be religiously oriented. There is no pure culture in the sense of being neutral religiously or without

positive or negative value ethically. Although the realization of values in a culture may seem on the surface to be concerned merely with the temporal and the material, this is appearance only, for man is a spiritual being destined for eternity, exhaustively accountable to his Creator-Lord. All that he does is involved in the whole of his nature as man.

Culture, however, does not include religion. The notion that it does is the basic error of practically all our cultural anthropologists, which fact may be ascertained by perusing casually any standard work on anthropology by such authors as Vander Leeuw, Malinowsky and others.

But the basic assumption underlying this position negates Christianity and is thoroughly naturalistic. For the position of the cultural anthropologist is that religion is simply a projection of the human spirit, an attempt to manipulate the unseen by magic, or, in any case, that man creates the gods of his own image, thus making it a cultural achievement. This is also the general attitude of the religious liberal, who uses religion for achieving man's ideal goals such as world peace....

The reason religion cannot be subsumed under culture is the fact that whereas man as a religious being transcends all his activities under the sun, culture is but one aspect of the sum total of these activities and their results in forming history. To divide life into areas of sacred and secular, letting our devotions take care of the former while becoming secular reformers during the week, is to fail to understand the true end of man.[6]

We need to understand that a man never can lay down his religion and act as a religionless person.

6. Van Til, H., *The Calvinistic Concept of Culture,* Presbyterian and Reformed Publishing Co., Nutley, N. J., 1972, p. 27.

He can have his religion changed, but he cannot act or think in a religionless manner, because religion is the governing principle of all he does, is and says. Religion is like the heart, out of it flow the issues of life, prejudicing all areas of human experience and thought (Proverbs 4:23).

This is re-affirmed by Jesus, when He taught that it is the heart that influences the thinking and behavior, and not vice versa (Mark 7:20). The implication, then, is clear: The Christian may never think or live as anything other than a Christian governed by the Word of God. He is never his own person, being "bought with a price."

He may not claim sovereign rights over his own opinion or behavior. He is a person under authority, who is striving to "bring every thought captive to Christ," even his political thoughts.

To attempt to act neutrally in any field of endeavor is to make the mistake of Eve, who assumed, that after God had spoken ("Don't eat!") and after Satan had spoken ("Do eat!"), she had to take a neutral position and decide for herself and by herself who spoke the truth. Thus, in a fallen condition, she, as the first humanist, pretended to have the autonomous ability and responsibility to determine for herself "good and evil" (Genesis 3:5). The Christian asks, "Who is man ever to take a neutral position to the command of the living God?" Neutrality is disobedience.

The other side of this coin should be obvious also. Since religious neutrality is a myth, those who profess to be such, have, in fact, laid aside their Christian presuppositions and have (unintentionally) taken up another religion. The humanists will not lay down their presuppositions, goals, and objectives. And when the Christian does so, he falls into humanists' well-laid trap. He, in reality, joins the humanist in striving for his goals and objectives. He adopts, in the political arena, the humanist's presupposition, which is the belief that man-in-community can solve his problems without reference to God or to His written revelation.

Religious neutrality in politics is especially dangerous, because of the far-reaching impact of legislation and laws. The source of law for a society is the god of that society. If the source of law is the Bible, then Almighty God is the God of that society.

On the other hand, if the source of law is man, then Man becomes the god, and that spells slavery and chaos for that society. As Rushdoony has written:

> Law is in every culture religious in origin. Because law governs man and society, because it establishes and declares the meaning of justice and righteousness, law is inescapably religious, in that it establishes in practical fashion the ultimate concerns of a culture. Accordingly, a fundamental and necessary premise in any and every study of law must be, first, a recognition of this religious nature of law.
>
> Second, it must be recognized that in any culture the source of law is the god of that society. If law has its source in man's reason, then reason is the god of that society. If the source is an oligarchy, or in a court, senate, or ruler, then that source is the god of that

system.

Modern humanism, the religion of the state, locates law in the state and thus makes the state, or the people as they find expression in the state, the god of the system. In Western culture, law has steadily moved away from God to the people (or the state) as its source, although the historical power and vitality of the West has been in biblical faith and law.

Third, in any society, any change of law is an explicit or implicit change of religion. Nothing more clearly reveals, in fact, the religious change in a society than a legal revolution. When the legal foundations shift from biblical law to humanism, it means that the society now draws its vitality and power from humanism, not from Christian theism.

Fourth, no disestablishment of religion as such is possible in any society. A Church can be disestablished, and a particular religion can be supplanted by another, but the change is simply to another religion. Since the foundations of law are inescapably religious, no society exists without a religious foundation or without a law-system which codifies the morality of its religion.

Fifth, there can be no tolerance in a law-system for another religion. *Toleration is a device used to introduce a new law-system as a prelude to a new intolerance.* Legal positivism, a humanistic faith, has been savage in its hostility to the biblical law-system and has claimed to be an "open" system.[7]

*"Religious neutrality in politics," is a subversive, revolutionary, and anti-Christian principle!*

The second fundamental weakness of this prin-

7. Rushdoony, R. J., *The Institutes of Biblical Law,* (Craig Press, 1973, Nutley, N. J.), p. 4

ciple is that it betrays two cardinal truths of the Christian religion: (1) The lordship of Christ over all of life; and (2) The all-embracing authority of the Bible, as the written Word of God.

One of the clearest teachings of Christianity is that Jesus Christ is King. He was hailed as such at His birth.[8] He professed to be such throughout His life.[9] He died as a King, in total control of the situation.[10] He arose from the grave as a majestic King.[11] He reigns over all today, and is working to establish His kingdom over all the earth.[12] He shall return at the end of history to consummate His reign.[13]

Faith is spoken of in terms of submission to His lordship.[14] Two things, then, become absolutely clear:

(1) The lordship of Christ is unlimited and unrestricted, i.e., it includes all areas of life without exception. There is no area of human life or in the entire creation that is not under His lordship and accountable to Him.

(2) Christ's lordship is of particular importance for the political realm. Revelation points out that Christ's rule includes the political arena, when He is called, *The ruler of the kings of the earth.*[15] Psalm

---

8. Luke 2:11
9. Mark 2:10,28
10. Colossians 2:15
11. Acts 2:32-36
12. I Corinthians 15:23-28
13. Philippians 2:9-11
14. Romans 10:9
15. Revelation 1:5

2 directly addresses civil governments and calls upon them to *Do homage to the Son, lest He become angry, and you perish in the way* .... The book of Acts indicates that the civil governments of Christ's day were intimidated by the political implications of the universal lordship of Christ.

The early Church certainly was aware of the conflict with Rome into which the issue of the lordship of Christ had brought them.

> And when they did not find them, they began dragging Jason and some brethren before the city authorities, shouting, "These men who have upset the world have come here also; and Jason has welcomed them, and they all act contrary to the decrees of Caesar, saying that there is another king, Jesus," (Acts 17:6-7).

The point appears to be obvious. Jesus Christ is the unrivaled monarch of the political process of the United States of America. Christians have the duty to declare His lordship in the American political arena; and they may not rest until His divine rights and absolute authority are recognized and submitted to in the executive, legislative, and judicial branches of our civil government at the national, state, and municipal levels.

For a Christian to seek anything less is to act as if Christ is something less than what He, in fact, is — King of kings and Lord of lords, Who possesses all authority and power in heaven and on earth.[16] Neutrality in politics is rebellion against the Lord

---

16. Matthew 28:18

Christ.

An example of proper zeal for the crown rights of Jesus Christ was Rev. James Henley Thornwell, who, in 1861, fought for the following preamble to be included in the constitution of the Confederacy:

> Nevertheless we, the people of these Confederate States, distinctly acknowledge our responsibility to God, and the supremacy of His Son, Jesus Christ, as King of kings and Lord of lords; and hereby ordain that no law shall be passed by the Congress of these Confederate States inconsistent with the will of God, as revealed in the Holy Scriptures.[17]

This brings us to the other cardinal truth at stake in this issue, which is the all-embracing authority of the Bible as the written Word of God. American Christians, since the landing of the pilgrim fathers, have been committed to the authority of biblical law as the only basis for a just, orderly and prospering society.[18] If Jesus Christ is Lord, He has given a law that is to be obeyed by all men and all nations.[19] Since Christ is King, it is impossible for a relationship to exist without revealed law. God's law was given to govern the entire life, thought and economy of a godly nation.

*Righteousness,* (i.e., conformity to biblical law,) *exalts a nation, but sin is a reproach to any people* (Proverbs 14:34).

God tells Israel in Deuteronomy 4:8 that there is

---

17. "Thornwell's Theocracy" in *Presbyterian Heritage,* Vol. 1, No. 1, published by Atlanta Christian Training Center, Atlanta, GA.
18. Deuteronomy 28-30
19. Exodus 20:1

no legal code or system of laws that is as just as the revealed law of God. Throughout the Old Testament, God judges Israel and many other nations, as nations, if they disregard or transgress biblical law.

In the New Testament, the civil government is said to be *the minister of God for good* and the *avenger who brings wrath upon the one who practices evil.* Both of these phrases are found in Romans 13:1-7. Their point is that it is the civil government's God-given responsibility to administer justice solely in terms of right and wrong.

For the Christian, as well as the writers of the New Testament, the only standard of right and wrong is the written Word of God. As a "minister" the civil government has the responsibility before God to administer His law. It does not have the right to legislate laws by fiat. Its authority is ministerial not legislative, according to the Bible.[20]

That makes the Bible of critical importance in politics, because justice is impossible, unless it is based upon the final authority of biblical law.[21] Jesus specifically says that the Scriptures, which can never be broken, were especially addressed to civil officials in John 10:35.

Consider these examples of the attitude the founding fathers of the United States had toward biblical law. First of all, we have a quotation from the "Fundamental Orders of Connecticut" (1638):

---

20. Study the book of Deuteronomy to see the all-embracing nature of God's law.

21. Proverbs 28:4,5; 29:4,14

...well knowing where a people are gathered together the Word of God requires that to maintain peace and union of such people there should be an orderly and decent government established according to God, to order and dispose of the affairs of the people at all seasons as occasion shall require; do therefore associate and conjoin ourselves to be as one public state or commonwealth; and do...enter into combination and confederation together, to maintain and preserve the liberty and purity of the gospel of our Lord Jesus Christ which we now profess...."[22]

Then we have a quotation from the New Haven Colony:

March 2, 1641, And according to the fundamental agreement made and published by full and general consent, when the plantation began and government was settled, that the judicial law of God given by Moses and expounded in other parts of Scripture, so far as it is a hedge and a fence to the moral law, and neither ceremonial nor typical nor had any reference to Canaan, hath an everlasting equity in it, and should be the rule of their proceedings. April 3, 1644: It was ordered that the judicial laws of God, as they were delivered by Moses...be a rule to all the courts in this jurisdiction in their proceeding against offenders...[23]

Last, we have a quotation from the "Address to the Reader" by Aspinwall in John Cotton's *Abstract of the Laws of New England* (1655):

This model far surpasseth all the municipal laws

---

22. Walton, R., *Fundamentals for American Christians*, Vol. 1, Plymouth Rock Foundation, N. H., p. 44
23. Rushdoony, *The Institutes of Biblical Law,* ( Craig Press, 1973, Nutley, N. J.), p. 1

and statutes of any of the Gentile nations and corporations under the scope of heaven. Wherefore I thought it not unmeet to publish it to the view of all, for the common good.... Judge equally and impartially, whether there be any laws in any state in the world, so just and equal as these be. Which, were they duly attended to, would undoubtedly preserve inviolable the liberty of the subject against all tyrannical and usurping powers.... This Abstract may serve for this use principally to show the complete sufficiency of the Word of God alone, to direct His people in judgment of all causes, both civil and criminal.... But the truth is, both they and we, and other Gentile nations, are loth to be persuaded to ... lay aside our old earthly forms of governments, to submit to the government of Christ."[24]

For the United States to survive, prosper and enjoy peace under the blessing of Almighty God, we must as a people and as a political structure confess that *the Lord is our Judge, the Lord is our Lawgiver, the Lord is our King; He will save us* (Isaiah 33:22).

The Christian must work toward the repeal of all laws that originate with humanism and toward the reinstitution of biblical law as the basis for the laws and legislation of the United States. Religious neutrality here amounts to the questioning of the justice and integrity of the revealed law of God.

Rushdoony makes the point dramatically, in his comments on Deuteronomy 6:4-9, known as the

---

24. Bahnsen, G., *Theonomy in Christian Ethics,* (Craig Press, 1977, Nutley, N. J.), p. 549

## SHEMA ISRAEL:

The first principle of the SHEMA ISRAEL is thus one God, one law. It is the declaration of an absolute moral order to which man must conform. If Israel cannot admit another god and another law-order, it cannot recognize any other religion or law-order as valid either for itself or for anyone else. Because God is one, truth is one.

All this illustrates a second principle of the SHEMA ISRAEL: one absolute, unchanging God means one absolute, unchanging law. Men's social applications and approximations of the righteousness of God may alter, vary, and waver, but the absolute law does not.

To speak of the law as "for Israel" but not for Christians is not only to abandon the law but also to abandon the God of the law. Since there is only one true God, and His law is the expression of His unchanging nature and righteousness, then to abandon the biblical law for another law-system is to change gods. The moral collapse of Christendom is a product of this current process of changing gods.

A third principle of the SHEMA ISRAEL is that one God, one law, requires one total, unchanging, and unqualified obedience. The meaning is that man must obey God totally, in any and every condition, with all his being. Since man is totally the creature of God, and since there is not a fiber of his being which is not the handiwork of God and therefore subject to the total law of God, there is not an area of man's life and being which can be held in reservation from God and His law.[25]

This should suffice to impress us with the fact that a Christian cannot enter the political arena and leave the law of God behind. To do so is to

---

25. Rushdoony, *The Institutes of Biblical Law,* p. 18

endanger his own welfare and to lay aside that guide which God gave to enhance the life, prosperity and peace of a nation according to Deuteronomy 28. Let it be made very clear, "Christ cannot be accepted if His sovereignty, His law, and His Word are denied."[26]

In conclusion, I trust it has been shown that the religious neutrality in politics principle is destructive to justice and to Christianity. It is another myth of secular humanism. It must be repudiated by all Christians.

It is my earnest prayer that Senator Mark Hatfield will re-evaluate his position in the light of the principles we have set forth here, insofar as they are in accordance with God's Word. I sincerely pray that, in rebuilding his political position in exclusively Christian and biblical terms, God will richly bless Senator Hatfield to be one of the powerful men in Congress whom God is using in the Christian reconstruction of the United States into a truly Christian Republic.

May all Christians everywhere re-commit themselves, by the grace of God, to pray for and diligently work toward the establishment of the crown rights of Jesus Christ over all the earth and the reconstruction of all aspects of American society and culture by the inerrant and all-sufficient Word of God in the power of the Holy Spirit to the glory of Almighty God.

---

26. Ibid. p. 667

CHAPTER SEVEN

# *The Keys and the Sword*
## *The Relation of Church and State*

America will rise to renewed greatness or fall to chaos and oblivion according to her answer to one question: What is the relation of Church and State? This is not an exaggeration, because the issue is sovereignty and salvation. Is one human institution sovereign over all others? Can any human institution bring salvation to a society? Who or what is the origin of social order? Whose word is the binding authority for Church and state? To whom do all institutions and individuals owe total allegiance — Christ or Caesar?

Humanism and Christianity give two entirely different answers to those questions. Humanism reserves sovereignty and salvation to man and the state. Christianity declares that they reside solely in the triune God.

> I am the Lord, that is my name; I will not give my glory to another (Isaiah 42:8).

> The Lord is our judge, the Lord is our lawgiver, the Lord is our king: He will save us (Isaiah 33:22).

> There is salvation in no one else; for there is no other name under heaven that has been given among men by which we must be saved (Acts 4:12).

These two religions are involved in a total war against each other for the United States of America including all her political, social, educational and ecclesiastical institutions. This conflict is anything but a scholastic, sectarian debate — it is a life and death issue. It is the difference between liberty and

slavery, between severe judgment by God and prosperity under God.

If man is the source of sovereignty and salvation,
then, he, by means of the state, will advance his
claim of total jurisdiction and total control in one
area after another, until the whole of human society, including the Church, is enslaved.

What, then, does the Bible, God's Word, teach us
about politics — about the relationship between
Church and State?

## There is a Proper Separation
## of Church and State

To say that there is a separation in no way implies
a radical antithesis between God and state, Christianity and state, morality and state, or Bible and
state. The humanists' understanding is that dramatic. There can be no such thing as philosophical,
religious or political neutrality in this area, or in
any area for that matter. **Religious neutrality in
politics is a myth the humanists try to impose
on the Christians, while they themselves are
never neutral.** Christians may never be neutral
for Jesus said that we are either for Him or against
Him; and between those two poles there is no neutral ground.

This separation is institutional and functional. In
the Bible there are clearly two separate institutions
with two different functions: the Church, (Matthew
16:18; 28:18) and the state, (civil government)
(Romans 13:1). The God-given function of the

Church is to carry out the Great Commission to disciple, baptize, and educate the nations (Matthew 28:19). The Church's task is a ministry of grace (II Corinthians 5:20).

The God-given function of the state is the administration of justice, i.e., the punishing of the lawless for the protection of the law-abiding, and the preservation of God's moral order (Romans 13:4; I Peter 2:13; I Timothy 2:1; Deuteronomy 16:17-18:20). The state's task is a ministry of justice.

This separation is firmly rooted in the Bible. In the Old Testament, we find the functional separation of Church and state in ancient Israel.[1] There was a distinction between the work of Moses, the civil leader, and Aaron, the levitical priest (Exodus 16:33; 29:1). During the period of restoration after the Babylonian Captivity, there was a clear distinction between Nehemiah the governor and Ezra the scribe.

Even after the Exodus and Mt. Sinai, the liturgical duties were assigned to the priests (Exodus 28-29), while the judicial and civil authority resided in the elders and heads of families (I Samuel 8:4; 10:20; II Samuel 3:17; 5:1). The only times that the levitical priests were involved in political matters were extraordinary cases (I Kings 1:38).

In the New Testament this separation is even more specifically defined. The Church, not the state, is given the power of the "keys," (Matthew

---

1. Bahnsen, Greg, *Theonomy In Christian Ethics,* ( Nutley, N.J., The Craig Press, 1977), pp. 401-433.

16:18), i.e., the authority to preach, teach, and apply the Word of God to all areas of life. This God-given power includes the authority to differentiate between right and wrong on the basis of biblical revelation. The power of the keys also includes the power "to shut the kingdom against the impenitent... by the Word... and to open it unto penitent sinners by the ministry of the gospel ..." (Matthew 18:17; John 20:21; II Corinthians 2:6).[2]

The state, not the Church, has been given the power of the "sword" (Romans 13:4). God has given the sword of execution and just force to be used in the faithful administration of godly justice within a nation. The God-given function of the state is to punish the lawless in terms of the moral law of God for the protection of the law-abiding citizens. The state is not to use the power of the sword to convert the populace, but to punish crime; and thereby, to maintain the peace and godly order. It is to use the sword so that the Church can have the freedom to use the keys. I Timothy 2:1-2 says: *I urge that... prayers... be made on behalf of... kings and all who are in authority, in order that we may lead a tranquil and quiet life in godliness and dignity.*

## There is a Proper Coherence of Church and State

They are closely related because they have something in common. To cohere means to be logically

---

2. *Westminster Confession Of Faith,* XXX,2

connected; to form a united or orderly whole. Coherence means the quality or state of the orderly relationship of parts.

This coherence in no way implies a blending of institutions and functions. Nor does it imply that the state is to use its power to force a particular Christian denomination upon its citizenry. Nor does it mean that all of society should be under the institutional Church.

The close relationship between Church and state exists because of what they have in common. They are both under God and accountable to His revealed Word. The head of the Church is not the state, it is God in Christ (Ephesians 1:22; 5:23). The head of the state is not the Church, it is God in Christ (Revelation 1:5; Proverbs 8:15; Daniel 2:20).

The Bible makes unmistakably clear that Christ's dominion includes the political arena, when He is called *the ruler of the kings of the earth,* in Revelation 1:5. In Psalm 2:10, God gives this command to all political authorities:

> Now, O kings, show discernment; take warning, O judges of the earth. Worship the Lord with reverence, and rejoice with trembling. Do homage to the Son, lest he become angry, and you perish in the way, for his wrath may soon be kindled.

Both Church and state are accountable to their *Origin,* which is the living God, Jehovah of Hosts. The Church was born in the mind of God and given to His people, as the body of Christ (Ephesians 1:3). Likewise, the civil government was born in the mind of God and given to mankind in order to maintain godly order (Genesis 9:6).

More specifically, Romans 13:1 asserts: *Let every person be in subjection to the governing authorities. For there is no authority except from God, and those which exist are established by God.* Therefore, the state's authority is derived from God, and not from the will of the majority.

The magistrate is therefore accountable to God as to how he administers that power. The civil government is totally responsible to its Creator for all its programs, actions, and legislation. It is obliged to govern solely in terms of God's will and God's authority. This is also true of the Church in its realm.

The point is this: a nation blessed by God is not a democracy, i.e., a nation governed by the majority. It is a republic, i.e., a nation ruled by a constitution based on the law of God. *Blessed is that nation whose God is Jehovah (Psalm 33:10).*

Both Church and state have specific *limitations* defined by God Himself in the Bible. They both are limited in their functions, powers, and the source of truth and law (Isaiah 33:22). God has not only ordained these two institutions, He has given them written directions in the Bible concerning their duties and how they are to carry them out justly and effectively so that His creation order may be respected and maintained. *They are limited in function.*

The state is to be a *terror* to the lawless, an *avenger* of God's wrath upon the lawless (Romans 13:3). Its functions do not include health, education and welfare. Those are the responsibilities of the family and the diaconate of the Church. The Church is to be a minister of the gospel — the bringer of the good news of Jesus Christ and His kingdom for a lost world, that belongs to God (Matthew 28:19).

They are *limited in power*. The Church does not have the authority to administer capital punishment, although it can administer Church discipline (Matthew 18:15), and even excommunication (I Corinthians 5:1-13). The state has the God-given authority to use the sword (legal, deadly force) and to tax (justly and biblically).

The authority of the state does not supercede the righteous use of power by the father, the elder, the headmaster, or the employer. The state may use its power only in the administration of civil sanctions and not in the creation by fiat of bureaucratic and governmental controls over a society, economy, Church, school, or family. Its power is not to be used to restrict or limit the God-given power of Christian individuals, families, Churches, schools, or businesses — in other words, Church and state are *limited in jurisdiction.*

The Church, directly under Christ her King, is an independent domain, even as the state is. It is a separate institution with its own functions and laws. The state has its own domain. It is to be the minister of justice for all. Both the Church and the state are responsible to Christ and His law. Neither Church nor state is man's supreme sovereign. Neither may usurp Christ's total authority over life.

They may exercise authority only within the jurisdiction given them by Christ, the King. To reject this limitation is political, cultural, and ecclesiastical suicide. The Church's jurisdiction is confined to preaching and teaching the Bible. The state's jurisdiction must be confined to the administration of justice as defined by biblical law.

This leads us to a final limitation on Church and state — their *source of truth and law*. Both Church and state must confess — *The Lord is our Lawgiver!* (Isaiah 33:22; James 4:12) Because there is only one God (Deuteronomy 6:4), there can be only one law. One absolute, unchanging God means one, absolute, unchanging law, binding on Church and state alike.

Deuteronomy 6:4-9 is "the declaration of an absolute moral order to which man must conform," writes R. J. Rushdoony.[3]

> Hear O Israel! The Lord is our God, the Lord is one! And you shall love the Lord your God with all your heart and with all your soul and with all your might. And these words, which I am commanding you today, shall be on your heart; and you shall teach them diligently to your sons....

Man's choice is either Christ, His law and "liberty and justice for all," or humanistic law and chaos.

To say that God's law is not relevant to modern American politics is to say that God is dead as far as

---

3. Rushdoony, R. J., *Institutes Of Biblical Law,* ( Nutley, N.J., The Craig Press, 1973), p. 18.

the most important issues of today's complex world are concerned. Because biblical law is a reflection of the character of God, to reject His law is to reject God Himself. To say it is irrelevant, is to say that God is irrelevant. Without the law of God at its foundation, a nation is ungovernable, and will eventually perish under God's judgment, unless it repents.

Christ cannot be accepted if His sovereignty, His law and His Word are denied!

It is only as the Church carries out her God-given task and as the state carries out its task, confining themselves to what God has revealed and commanded, that our nation will know peace and prosperity under God's blessing.

If the Church is not sounding forth faithfully and powerfully the Word of the Lord, a nation will have no direction and guidance. If the state is not faithfully administering the justice of the Lord, the Church will be the first to suffer when freedom begins to disappear.

The only gospel that the Church may administer is that revealed in the written revelation of Almighty God. The only standard of justice the state may administer is that revealed in the Word of God. Both Church and state are called *ministers* in the New Testament (Romans 13:3).

A minister of the gospel does not create doctrines by fiat: he administers what God has written. The same is true for the civil magistrate — the minister of justice — he may not make laws by fiat. His authority is ministerial, not legislative. His legislation must be based on what God has written. He is to administer God's law reflected in the nation's constitution, not to create laws of his own making.

May all Christians everywhere re-commit themselves, by the grace of God, to pray for and work toward the establishment of the crown rights of Jesus Christ over all the earth and the Christian reconstruction of all aspects of American society and politics by the infallible Word of God and the invincible Spirit of God to the glory of the triune God.

May we not rest until we see, under the Lord's blessing, Christian individuals in Christian families and Christian Churches and Christian schools, and Christian businesses in a truly Christian Republic with genuinely Christian elected officials and Christian judges practicing biblical law and passing Christian legislation.

May that day come when our beloved nation will publicly and honestly confess: "We the people of the United States of America, distinctly acknowledge our responsibility to God and the supremacy of His Son, Jesus Christ, as King of kings and Lord of lords: and hereby ordain that no law shall be passed by the Congress of these United States inconsistent with the will of God, as revealed in the Holy Scriptures."[4]

---

4. James H. Thornwell in *Presbyterian Heritage* , Vol. I, No. I, Atlanta Christian Training Seminars.

CHAPTER EIGHT

# *The Meaning of the Life and Death of Larry McDonald*

This chapter first appeared as an article in
*The Counsel Of Chalcedon,*
Vol. V, No. 8, October, 1983.

If, when you think of Larry McDonald, you think only of anti-communism, you have misunderstood Larry McDonald. The all-consuming calling and goal of his life was to preserve and reinstate the United States Constitution *and* the distinctively biblical heritage that gave it birth and filled it with meaning. He lived and died defending it against any who conspire to overturn it, both inside and outside our nation.

Larry understood that the preservation and advancement of the way of life of that heritage, and the rule of law of that Constitution are absolutely essential to liberty and justice for all. For a nation to guarantee for itself security, liberty and prosperity under God's blessing, the civil government of that nation must restrict itself to the faithful administration of the function God has assigned it in the Bible as reflected in our Constitution — the administration of justice — not of health, education and welfare, but the punishment of the lawless for the protection of the lawful.

> For rulers are not a cause of fear for good behavior, but for evil. Do you want to have no fear of authority? Do what is good, and you will have praise from the same; for it is a minister of God to you for good. But if you do what is evil, be afraid; for it does not bear the sword for nothing; for it is a minister of God, an avenger who brings wrath upon the one who practices evil (Romans 13:3-4).

This clearly indicates that the maintenance of a

strong and effective defence program, sufficient to protect the citizenry from any lawless invader, is essential to godly rule. To do otherwise — to allow the nation's families to stand in a vulnerable position — is irresponsible and immoral. This God-given power of the sword is bestowed upon the state, so that it can be effective as *an avenger* who brings God's wrath upon the one who practices evil.

In other words, as a civil government is faithful to God in administering true justice and godly restitution, God takes His holy vengeance upon those who try to overthrow His moral order in creation. A nation that sheaths that sword because of partiality, that surfeits it in lawless cruelty, that retires it because of humanistic sentimentality, that denies its right of existence, or that wields it beyond its limited domain stands condemned by Almighty God.

Larry understood that, when the authors of the U.S. Constitution spoke of law, they meant the law of God as revealed in the Bible. I have heard him say many times that we must refute humanistic, relativistic law with biblical law. This view was affirmed by the Congress of the United States on October 4, 1982, when both Houses passed Public Law 97-280, which states that "Biblical teachings inspired concepts of civil government that are contained in our Declaration of Independence and the Constitution of the United States," that "the Bible is 'the rock on which our Republic rests'," that "the history of our Nation clearly illustrates the value of voluntarily applying the teachings of the scriptures in the lives of individuals, families, and societies," that "the renewing of our knowledge of and faith in God through Holy Scripture can strengthen us as a nation," that Congress recognizes "the normative influence the Bible has been for our Nation, and our national need to study and apply the teachings of the Holy Scriptures."

In Romans 13, God describes the state as *a minister of God*. Both Church and state are designated *ministers* in the New Testament. As a Church has no authority to create doctrines by fiat, so the state has no authority from God to administer any other standard of public justice, than the law of God.

Its authority is ministerial, not creatively legislative. Its legislation must be based on the laws of God. If the state is not faithfully administering justice in terms of biblical law, the Church will be the first to suffer, when freedom begins to disappear.

The reason for this is clear: the source of law for any society is the god of that society. And that god will tolerate no rival gods. The uncompromising Christian Church is a threat to a state that considers itself to be god.

Show me where a nation derives its laws, and I will show you the god it worships, regardless of what is written on its coins.

Therefore, the issue facing our nation, the issue that is polarizing us, is not that of more laws and regulations versus less laws and regulations. It is a deeper issue — are we to be governed by man's law or by God's law. If man is god, slavery and chaos reign. If the Lord is God, peace reigns. *Blessed is that nation whose God is the Lord.*

If, when you think of the murder of Larry McDonald, you feel only anger toward the Soviets, who murdered him, you have missed the deeper significance of that incident for your future as an American.

Throughout our history, our fathers have believed in Divine Providence — that God's guiding hand rests upon the affairs of nations and men. This produced in those who believed it a sense of confidence in the future and a spur to responsibility. Today, that same faith in Providence should produce in us a certain solemnity.

Our nation, at all levels, is in a state of revolt against that God of Providence. We have mixed our silver with dross. We have made alliances with those who represent anti-Christian law-orders. We have judges more concerned with revolutionary social change than with the administration of simple and godly justice. We have succumbed to debt-oriented living. We have lived for leisure and affluence, rather than for hard work, useful productivity, and the glory of God.

We have looked to man and his institutions for salvation, for cradle-to-grave security, rather than to the living God through Jesus Christ. We have abandoned our Christian heritage and culture that made our nation the greatest on earth. We have downgraded the family, and given ourselves to immorality and pornography.

We are robbing the Church and Christian school of more and more of their rights and freedoms. We have changed gods, and our new, impotent gods are failing us. We have elected men to office who have no commitment to God and no sense of accountability to Him and to His law for legislation.

And now everybody is beginning to see the bankruptcy of these new and false gods. Everybody knows the emperor has no clothes. We are enraged at the murder of 269 people by the Soviets, but we are not equally outraged at the murder of millions of unborn babies by Americans.

These heinous national and personal sins bring us under the severe judgment of Almighty God.

> Therefore the Lord God of hosts, the Mighty One of Israel declares: "I will be relieved of my adversaries, and avenge myself of my foes. I will also turn my hand against you, and will smelt away your dross with lye, and will remove your alloy. Then I will restore your judges as at the first and your counselors as at the beginning ...." (Isaiah 1:24-26).

How can one tell whether or not God has begun to bring down His judgment upon a society? Are there any signs that judgment has already begun? The answer is to be found in Isaiah 3:1-5:

> Behold, the Lord God of hosts is going to remove... both supply and support... (He is going to remove) the mighty  man and the warrior, the judge and the prophet, the diviner and the elder, the captain of fifty and the honorable man, the counselor and the expert artisan, and the skillful enchanter. And I will make mere lads rule over them, and the people will be

oppressed, each one by another, and each one by his neighbor; the youth will storm against the elder, and the inferior against the honorable.

So then, what are the signs that God has begun to judge the United States for our revolt against Him? He is depriving our nation of its most necessary means of life, politically, militarily, economically, agriculturally, socially, educationally, morally, and religiously. All that our nation trusts in — both good and bad — all it leans on is being taken away.

We are watching a drying up of our national health, vitality and hope. Along with this is the removal of good leadership, guides we can trust, leaders who will not betray us, like Congressman Lawrence Patton McDonald. The feeling in this congressional district is that the one man who would never let us down, and who would always lead us in the right way is gone. Much of the remaining leadership is, as Isaiah 3 describes, lacking wisdom, maturity, courage, resolve, understanding, and a sense of direction.

Many have no appreciation of the heritage of our past and no commitment to our future as a Christian Republic. They live and legislate only for the present. This attitude breeds irresponsibility and short-sighted, self-centered planning. As one of them said, when questioned about the long-term consequences of his inflationary policies on our grandchildren, "In the long-run, I will be dead."

This Bible chapter goes on to describe additional signs of God's judgment upon a nation. There will be a rise of anarchy, confusion, and a loss of unity and freedom. Responsible men will abdicate the places of power, and women will have to take the reins. There will be a moral decline among women, as well as men, as illustrated in feminism and the ERA. Then will come the horrors of war, and with that, the tragic disappearance of men and boys. In a nation where God is dead, or considered irrelevant, man is dead.

This is our future unless we truly repent of our sins individually and nationally. Isaiah 1:16-20 says:

> Wash yourselves, make yourselves clean; remove the evil of your deeds from my sight. Cease to do evil, learn to do good; seek justice, reprove the ruthless; defend the orphan, plead for the widow. Come now, and let us reason together, says the Lord, though your sins are as scarlet, they will be as white as snow; though they are red like crimson, they will be like wool. If you consent and obey, you will eat of the best of the land; but if you refuse and rebel, you will be devoured by the sword. Truly, the mouth of the Lord has spoken.

God presents you, ladies and gentlemen, with two alternatives: obey Him and prosper or disobey Him and be devoured by the sword!

**Political leaders:** Repent of your sins that have brought us to this moment. Rededicate yourself to the proposition that: *The Lord is our judge. The Lord is our lawgiver. The Lord is our king. He will save us* (Isaiah 33:22). Bow before the supremacy of the Son of God. See to it that no law shall be passed in these United States inconsistent with the will of God as revealed in Holy Scriptures.

**Church leaders:** Repent of your sins that have brought us to this moment. Rededicate yourself to the bold and practical preaching of the whole counsel of God which is revealed in the Bible and which applies to every area of life. Do not fear men. Be confident that the power of the Word of God can and will overturn all the "isms" of men. Preach *all* the Bible and *only* the Bible. Recover your neglected role of prophet. Confront the political institutions and power brokers of our day with their accountability to the law of God and to Jesus Christ, who claimed to be "the ruler of the kings of the earth." Stand with Jeremiah of old, with the Word of God in your mouth and, like a hammer, break the rock of humanism and communism to pieces!

**Citizens of the United States:** Repent of your sins that have brought us to this moment. Quit looking to the civil government for salvation and sustenance. Turn from your apathy and involve yourself in the battle for the survival of the United States. Repent of your debt-oriented living. Repent of setting as the priority of your life — comfort and affluence. Be willing to give all you are and all you have to Christ and to the advance of His kingdom.

In the last speech Larry McDonald delivered, the Saturday night before his death, he said that, if we are going to win this war before us, we must give ourselves selflessly and relentlessly to the advancement of the causes of God, of righteousness and of truth until one of two things happen — we win or we are laid in our graves.

The last thing Larry asked me to do for him was to write some material he could use to motivate Christians to become more involved, consistently and perseveringly, in the critical battle for our future, and the future of our children. That is what I have tried to do for him and to the glory of God.

> If Christ is really king, exercising original and immediate jurisdiction over the State as really as He does over the Church, it follows necessarily that the general denial or neglect of His rightful Lordship, any prevalent refusal to obey that Bible which is the open law-book of His kingdom, must be followed by political and social, as well as moral and religious ruin.

> If professing Christians are unfaithful to the authority of their Lord in their capacity as citizens of the State, they cannot expect to be blessed by the indwelling of the Holy Spirit in their capacity as members of the Church.

> The kingdom of Christ is one, and cannot be divided in life or in death. If the Church languishes, the State cannot be in health; and if the State rebels against its Lord and King, the Church cannot enjoy His favor. If the Holy Spirit is withdrawn from the Church, He is not present in the State; and if He, the only "Lord of life," be absent, then all is impossible, and the elements of society lapse backward to primeval night and chaos.

> In the name of your own interests I plead with you; in the name of your treasure-houses and barns, of your rich farms and cities, of your accumulations in the past and your hopes in the future — I charge you, you never will be secure if you do not faithfully maintain all the crown-rights of Jesus the King of men.

In the name of your children and their inheritance of the precious Christian civilization you in turn have received from your sires; in the name of the Christian Church, — I charge you that its sacred franchise, religious liberty, cannot be retained by men who in civil matters deny their allegiance to the King.

In the name of your own soul and its salvation; in the name of the adorable victim of that bloody and agonizing sacrifice whence you draw all your hopes of salvation; by Gethsemane and Calvary; I charge you, citizens of the United States, afloat on your wide sea of politics, there is another King, one Jesus; the safety of the state can be secured only in the way of humble and whole-souled loyalty to His person and of obedience to His law.[1]

*Editor's note:* Dr. Larry McDonald of Atlanta, Georgia, was a U. S. Congressman at the time of his death. He was aboard Korean Airlines Flight 007 when it was shot down by Communist Russia. Two hundred and sixty-nine people lost their lives. Since neither the plane nor the bodies were ever found, there is some speculation that the plane actually landed and Russia has kept secret the facts surrounding this ill-fated flight. Even as the United States — once again — bails out a failing Communist system, we have not demanded that the truth be revealed regarding this incident.

---

1. Hodge, A. A., *Popular Lectures On Theological Themes,* (Philadelphia, Presbyterian Board of Education, 1887), pp. 285-287.

CHAPTER NINE

# *What are You Doing About the American Holocaust?*

This chapter first appeared as an article in
*The Counsel of Chalcedon,*
Vol. X, No. 10, December, 1988

A holocaust is a massive and gruesome destruction of human life. The first great holocaust on record is Pharoah's slaughter of infants recorded in Exodus 1:15. The New Testament holocaust is the slaughter of infants under Herod (Matthew 2:16). Modern holocausts have taken place under Hitler, Stalin, and Mao. It is estimated that 150 million people have died in this century due to Communistic totalitarianism. We are also going through a new holocaust in the United States.

The U. S. Supreme Court has made two landmark decisions which have increased the massive and gruesome destruction of human life in America. In 1973, in the Roe vs. Wade decision, the Supreme Court created, out of nothing, a woman's right to abortion on demand for her own convenience. According to that decision, unborn babies are not "persons," therefore not under the protection of the law. The court sovereignly and irresponsibly declared that "when life begins" is not the issue. Justice Byron White called this decision "an exercise of raw judicial power."

In 1983, the Supreme Court rendered a decision concerning restrictions on abortion clinics in Ohio, Missouri and Virginia. Dissenting Justices were Sandra Day O'Connor, William Rehnquist and Byron White. This decision struck down state restrictions on abortions as unconstitutional. Faye Wattleton, president of the Planned Parenthood

Federation of America, as quoted in *The Washington Times,* June 16, 1983, said concerning this decision: "We commend the court for its steadfast commitment to defending the rights of each of us, and for its compassionate consideration of fundamental human needs."

Let's look at the "compassion" of the Supreme Court. When we do, we will find that *the compassion of the wicked is cruel,* to quote the Book of Proverbs. In that 1983 decision, the Court *struck down* state laws that attempted to require that:

• Abortions performed after the first three months of pregnancy be performed in full-care hospitals.

• All minors get the consent of a parent or of a juvenile court before having an abortion.

• A doctor reads a specific description of the fetus and the abortion procedure to a woman desiring an abortion.

• Doctors wait 24 hours after a woman signs a consent form before conducting an abortion.

• Fetal remains be disposed of in a "humane and sanitary manner."

(*The Washington Times,* June 16, 1983, p. 12a.)

Because of those two decisions, many millions of unborn babies have been legally murdered in the United States. These babies have no ability or "right" to protect themselves and have few people trying to defend them. This is our modern American Holocaust — the issue of the 1990's. This one issue will surely bring God's swift and decisive judgment on us unless we repent, for God has said: *The Lord hates... hands that shed innocent blood ...* (Proverbs 6:16,17).

In *The Atlanta Journal,* June 18, 1981, an article appeared with this heading: "Defective Twin Fetus Killed by MDs." It reported that:

> Doctors punctured the heart of a defective five-month-old fetus and left it to wither away in the womb beside its normal twin because, the doctors said, the mother decided she "could not face the burden of caring for an abnormal child."

It went on to say that:

> The doctors said that "out of an abundance of caution" they obtained an opinion from a New York state court acknowledging their right to perform the operation. "We wanted to confirm from the court that the parents had the right to do this on behalf of the normal fetus," Kereny said.

But what of the rights of and compassion for the fetus with Down's Syndrome? *The compassion of the wicked is cruel!* Moreover, it appears that the doctors involved considered the state court the bestower of rights, the lord and giver of life. The Supreme Court giveth and the Supreme Court taketh away, blessed be the name of the Supreme Court.

The Newsletter of the Georgia Right to Life Committee, May, 1983, carried the following headlines: "14 Live Births in 3 Years at Midtown Hospital." The article pointed out:

> According to statistics on file at the Georgia State Department of Human Resources, a total of 14 live births

occurred at Atlanta's Midtown Hospital over a three-year period, from 1980-1982. — Certificates of death for the 14 aborted babies indicate both the approximate interval between the onset of the abortion process and the death of the child, as well as the length of time the child lived. — The maximum time period an aborted baby sustained life outside the womb in the three-year study of Midtown was 13 hours and five minutes. According to the death certificate, dated April of 1981, the immediate cause of death was "pulmonary insufficiency, therapeutic abortion."

*The compassion of the wicked is cruel!*

Statistics in *A.L.L. About Issues,* newsletter of the American Life Lobby, June 1983, showed that abortions outnumber live births in 14 U. S. cities. *The compassion of the wicked is cruel!*

How are we to evaluate these grisly facts? For Christians, the real question is: What does God say about abortion in the Bible? Consider carefully the following biblical information:

> For He who has set the limits to our life has at the same time entrusted to us its care: He has provided means and helps to preserve it: He has also made us able to foresee dangers; that they may not overwhelm us unaware, He has offered precautions and remedies. Now it is very clear to us what our duty is: Thus if the Lord has committed to us the protection of our life, our duty is to protect it; if He offers helps, to use them; if He forewarns us of dangers, not to plunge headlong; if He makes remedies available, not to neglect them.[1]

This pro-life view of John Calvin, as representa-

---

1. Calvin, John, *Institutes of the Christian Religion* (I, 17,4).

tive of biblical Christianity, is rooted in the fact that God is the Creator of all human life and the Re-creator of life in Christ (John 17:2). God made man and woman in His own image (Genesis 1:27), to reflect His character and glory. Jesus Christ came to restore that image which had been marred by sin (Ephesians 4:24; Colossians 3:10). This gives all human life sanctity, in other words, a sacred inviolability defined by God's Word. Therefore, human life, in all its phases, must be treated with dignity and respect. *Thou shalt not kill* means, positively, that we are to preserve, enhance, and protect the lives of others.

Because God made man in His own image, He gives to human life His own special protection. He interprets assaults on human life as audacious assaults on Himself. Genesis 9:6-7 brings this out clearly:

> Whoever sheds man's blood, by man, his blood shall be shed; For in the image of God He made man. And as for you, be fruitful and multiply; Populate the earth abundantly and multiply in it.

And Jesus Himself said to Saul of Tarsus en route to Damascus to arrest Christians, *Saul, Saul, why are you persecuting Me?* (Acts 9:4). Human life is so sacred to God, that if a man takes another life unlawfully, that man would have to forfeit his own life.

The question of the hour is this: Is the unborn child covered by God's special protection? Is the unborn child a human person in God's image?

The Bible is clear in its answers to these crucial questions. It leaves no doubt about the continuity of personhood which includes the unborn child. The Bible teaches that at conception (more accurately, at fertilization), the unborn child is a human person in the image of God, and, therefore, under His special protection. This point is made in a variety of convincing ways:

1. The express statement on the beginning of human life (Job 3:3).
2. The continuity of personhood from conception through adulthood (Psalm 139:13-16).
3. The continuity of sinfulness from conception through adulthood (Psalm 51:5).
4. The continuity of human experiences from conception through adulthood (Luke 1:15, 41,44).
5. The nature of conception as a gracious act of God (I Samuel 1:19).
6. The case-law governing abortion (Exodus 21:22-25).

## 1. The Bible Identifies the Beginning of Human Life as Conception.

God defines man (Hebrew, "Adam") as *the image of God,* Genesis 1:26, thereby exalting him as the crown of creation (Psalm 8:5). This first individual man is named "Adam," and from the side of this man (Hebrew, "iysh" in 2:23), God took a rib to create an individual woman, named Eve (Genesis 2:23). Having been given the divine gift and mandate of procreativity (Genesis 1:28), *Adam knew his wife, Eve, and she conceived and gave birth to Cain,* (Genesis 4:1).

When she gave birth to her child she made this confession of faith, *with the help of the Lord, I have brought forth a man,* "iysh", (Genesis 4:1). Notice two things about this confession. First, Eve confessed that conception and birth result from the sovereign activity of God in human sexuality. Second, this child is to be viewed as "man," — as divine image-bearer from birth.

The Bible, however, goes back even beyond birth and identifies the unborn child as God's image-bearer from conception. In Job 3:3, we find Job saying: *Let the day perish on which I was to be born, and the night which said, "A man* (Hebrew "geber") *is conceived."*

Simply noting Job's depression, let us go on and point out that Job considered his humanness to have begun the very night in which he was conceived. The Hebrew word for "man" or "boy" (NASV) in this verse is not the more general word for man as "iysh" and "adam," but the more specific and distinct word, "geber." "This word specifically relates to a male at the height of his powers. As such it depicts humanity at its most competent and capable level," (page 148-149 in *Theological Wordbook of the Old Testament,* vol. I, R. Laird Harris, Ed., Moody Press, Chicago, 1980).

This word, geber, distinctly denotes the humanness of man in his exalted position as the crown of creation (Psalm 34:8; 37:23), and the image of God. ("Adam," "iysh," and "geber" are used interchange-ably for "man" the divine image-bearer, Psalm 37:23, 37: 32:2). In Job 3:3, where Job refers to himself at his conception, he considers himself to be fully human, fully bearing God's image. This latter point is obvious also from the fact that a form of the word, geber, is used several times in reference to God as one of His perfections (Job 12:13, Proverbs 8:14; Isaiah 9:6). Hence, the Creator's character is reflected ("imaged") in man, His creature, from con-ception onward.

## 2. The Bible Identifies a Continuity of Personhood from Conception Through Adulthood.

Psalm 139:13-16 is central to any discussion of abortion.

> For Thou didst form my inward parts;
> Thou didst weave me in my mother's womb.
> I will give thanks to Thee,
> For I am fearfully and wonderfully made;
> Wonderful are Thy works,
> And my soul knows it very well.
> My frame was not hidden from Thee,
> When I was made in secret,
> And skillfully wrought in the depths of the earth.
> Thine eyes have seen my unformed substance;
> And in Thy book they were all written,
> The days that were ordained for me,
> When as yet there was not one of them.

Notice two emphases of this passage. First of all

life, including pre-natal life, is viewed as a gift from God. ("Unformed substance" in Hebrew is "golem," literally translated embryo or fetus.) Second, David continually emphasizes the continuity of his personhood from his embryonic existence to his adult existence. In 139:13, he says, *Thou didst form me in my mother's womb.* In 139:15, he adds, *My frame was not hidden from Thee, when I was made in secret.* David could speak of himself as "I" outside the womb, and inside the womb as well, pointing to the fact that he existed as a personal human being even in his embryonic state.

### 3. The Bible Identifies a Continuity of Sinfulness from Conception Through Adulthood.

In Psalm 51:5, we read: *Surely I have been a sinner from birth, sinful from the time my mother conceived me.*

Besides emphasizing again the continuity of David's human personhood from conception, David also points out that he has been a sinner, not only since his birth, but since his conception. He was conceived a sinner, having inherited a sinful nature from his parents on back to Adam (Romans 5:12). Now the point is this: Only human beings sin! Sub-human creatures do not sin. Only those who have a spiritual, as well as a physical aspect of their being, sin (Genesis 2:7). Only those in the image of God transgress their Maker's will. Only those created in knowledge, righteousness, holiness and dominion are capable of sinning. Hence being a sinner from conception, David is saying he was a human being in the image of God from conception, in need of God's mercy.

### 4. The Bible Identifies a Continuity of Human Experiences from Conception Through Adulthood.

Although we often attribute human emotions and experiences to sub-human creatures out of sentimental attachment to them, there are some joys and experiences that are unique to human beings. For instance, the rich blessing of the *filling of the Holy Spirit* (Ephesians 5:18), is one of the highest spiritual blessings that a regenerate image-bearer can experience. Also the joy that a regenerate person experiences caused by the power of the gospel of Jesus Christ is also a unique blessing (Luke 2:10).

The New Testament teaches that unborn children are capable of experiencing these two blessings while still in the womb. In Luke 1:15, we find the angel prophesying to Zacharias concerning the birth of his son, John the Baptist. He announces that, *He will be great in the sight of the Lord... and he will be filled with the Holy Spirit, while yet in his mother's womb*. Later in Luke 1:44, the unborn John, at the announcement of the conception of the Messiah, is said to experience "joy" — *For, behold, when the sound of your greeting reached my ears, the baby leaped in my womb for joy*. Being capable of being "filled with the Spirit," and experiencing "gospel-joy" while yet unborn, confirms that John was not only fully human in the womb, but also regenerate in the womb.

### 5. The Bible Describes Conception as a Gracious Gift and Work of God.

In the Bible, conception and birth are never viewed as mere human happenings. The Bible emphasizes the sovereign activity of God in conception and birth. Apart from this sovereign intervention of God, conception does not take place. Conception must be viewed, in the light of the Bible, as a blessed gift from God Himself.

It is written that in the pregnancy of Sarah, *The Lord did for Sarah as He had promised* (Genesis 21:1-2). In Genesis 30:1-2 we hear Jacob rebuking Rachel for her complaint against him for her childlessness: *Am I in the place of God, who has withheld from you the fruit of the womb?*

In I Samuel 1:19, we find Hannah conceiving because *the Lord remembered her.* Job confesses that God "made" him in the womb (Job 31:15), and that *the Spirit of God has made me, and the breath of the Almighty gives me life* (Job 33:4). It is for these reasons that the Psalms declare *it is He* (God) *who has made us, and not we ourselve.* (Psalms 100:3). And, *children are a gift of the Lord; the fruit of the womb is a reward* (Psalms 127:3).

In the light of these verses, we can only conclude that: "It would be a willful act of defiance against the creator intentionally to kill an unborn child whose conception is so intimately a divine as well as a human act." (Report of the Ad Interim Committee on Abortion, Minutes of the Sixth General Assembly of the Presbyterian Church in America, 1978.)

## 6. The Case-law Governing Abortion: Exodus 21:22-25

> If men who are fighting hit a pregnant woman and she gives birth prematurely, but there is no serious injury, the offender must be fined whatever the woman's husband demands and the court allows. But if there is serious injury, you are to take life for life, eye for eye, tooth for tooth, hand for hand, foot for foot, burn for burn, wound for wound, bruise for bruise.

This passage does not teach that the unborn child is of less value than a child after birth, as the report on abortion by the Presbyterian Church in the United States (1973) inaccurately maintains. The following exposition of the passage is taken from the report on abortion by the Presbyterian Church in America (1978):

> The term YELED in verse 22 never refers elsewhere to a child lacking recognizable human form, or to one incapable of existing outside the womb. The possibility of such a usage here, as the interpretation in question requires, is still further reduced by the fact that if the writer had wanted to speak of an undeveloped embryo or fetus there may have been the terminology available to him. There was the term GOLEM (Psalm 129:16) which means "embryo, fetus." But in cases of death of an unborn child, scripture regularly designates him, not by YELED, not even by GOLEM, but by NEFEL (Job 3:16; Psalm 58:8; Ecclesiastes

6:3), "one untimely born." The use of YELED in verse 22, therefore, indicates that the child in view is not the product of a miscarriage, as the interpretation in question supposes; at least this is the most natural interpretation in the absence of decisive considerations to the contrary.

Further, the verb YATZA in verse 22 ("go out," translated "depart" in KJV) does not in itself suggest the death of the child in question, and is ordinarily used to describe normal births (Genesis 25:26; 38:28-30; Job 3:11; 10:18; Jeremiah 1:5; 20:18). With the possible exception of Numbers 12:12, which almost certainly refers to a stillborn, it never refers to a miscarriage. The Old Testament term normally used for miscarriage and spontaneous abortion, both in humans and in animals, is not "YATZA" but SKAKOL (Exodus 23:26; Hosea 9:14; Genesis 31:38; Job 2:10; II Kings 2:19,21; Malachi 3:11). The most natural interpretation of the phrase WEYATZ'U YELADHEYHA, therefore, will find in it not an induced miscarriage, not the death of an unborn child, but an induced premature birth, wherein the child is born alive, but ahead of the anticipated time.

We should also note that the term "ason" (harm), found in both verse 22 and verse 23 is indefinite in its reference. The expression "lah" ("to her"), which would restrict the harm to the woman in distinction from the child, is missing. Thus the most natural interpretation would regard the "harm" as pertaining either to the woman or to the child. Verse 22 therefore describes a situation where neither mother or child is "harmed" — i.e., where the mother is uninjured and the child is born alive. Verse 23 describes a situation where some harm is done — *either* to mother *or* to child or *both*.... An induced miscarriage could hardly be described as a situation where there is "no harm." Verse 22, therefore, describes, not an induced miscarriage, but an induced premature birth.

In this light, translations using the word "miscarriage" or its equivalent are both inaccurate and misleading. The intent of this passage appears in the following paraphrase: "And if men fight together and hurt a pregnant woman so that her child is born prematurely, yet neither mother or child is harmed, he shall be surely fined, according as the woman's husband shall lay upon him; and he shall pay as the judges determine. But if either mother or child is harmed, then thou shall give life for life, eye for eye, tooth for tooth, hand for hand, foot for foot, etc."

## Conclusion

The view that "abortion is not a desirable solution although it may be at times a necessary option," (Presterian Church of the United States "Report on Abortion," 1973) is in flat contradiction to the Word of God. To hold that view or to recommend abortion for socio-economic or psychological reasons is flagrantly to disregard the command of God protecting human life, because of the sanctity He gives it — *Thou shall not commit murder.*

"The Word of God affirms throughout the continuity of personhood both before and after birth. Abortion, the intentional killing of an unborn child, is to destroy that continuity. Abortion would terminate the life of an individual, a bearer of God's image who is being divinely formed and prepared for a God-given role in the world." (P.C.A. "Report on Abortion," 1978).

According to the Bible, abortion is murder. And murder is a capital crime.

God's hatred for abortionists is clear in that He

says He *hates... hands that shed innocent blood...* (Proverbs 6:16,17).

> The Lord says this, "For three sins of Ammon, even for four, I will not turn back my wrath. Because he ripped open the pregnant women of Gilead in order to extend his borders, I will set fire to the walls of Rabbah..." (Amos 1:13-15).

This is strong language. But we must feel God's contempt for abortion. We must recognize fully its heinousness and criminality. What then must our response be to this modern holocaust — the slaughter of the unborn? The Bible answers in Proverbs 24:10-12:

> If you falter in times of trouble,
> how small is your strength!
> Rescue those being led away to death;
> hold back those staggering toward slaughter.
> If you say, "But we knew nothing about this,"
> does not he who weighs the heart perceive it?
> Does not he who guards your life know it?
> Will he not repay each person according to what
> he has done?

In obedience to this God-inspired proverb, let us:
1. Realize the urgency of the situation — each year over one-and-one-half million unborn babies are aborted.
2. Realize that God's judgment rests on a nation that allows or condones murder, unless it truly repents. Numbers 35:33 warns: *So shall you not pollute the land and no expiation can be made for the land for the blood that is shed on it except by the blood of him who shed it.*
3. Communicate to elected officials and legislators

that God has His moral standards that we must honor, and that one of those standards condemns abortion.

4. Educate and organize your Christian friends to stand unashamedly for the sanctity of human life in their own communities and before their state legislators.

5. Establish and get involved with a local chapter of the Christian Action Council, 422 C Street, NE, Washington, DC 20002.

6. Keep yourself informed by subscribing to the Christian Action Council's excellent newsletter, *Action Line,* at the above address.

7. Involve yourself in crisis pregnancy ministries in your local Church, ministering to women with unwanted pregnancies.

8. Check with local Christian adoption agencies for the possibility of adopting an otherwise unwanted newborn.

9. Consider taking unwed pregnant girls into your home.

10. Teach your children about marital sexuality, the sanctity of human life, and the joy and beauty of pre-marital chastity.

11. Check with your OB-GYN and find out if he does abortions. If he does, drop him and encourage other Christians to do the same.

12. Have funerals for children who die before birth.

13. Beware of the March of Dimes' involvement in the modern holocaust. For documentation write: Director of the U. S. Coalition for Life, P. O. Box

315, Export, PA 15632, or call 412/327-8878.

14. Identify Planned Parenthood Federation as an accomplice in the holocaust.

15. Write letters to editors of newspapers and elected officials about the holocaust.

16. Picket abortion clinics.

17. Pray Psalm 58 against abortionists.

18. Distribute copies of this book to Christians, ministers, government officials and others. Send $8.95 each (includes postage and handling) to Covenant House Books, P. O. Box 4690, Sevierville, TN 37864. (Quantity discounts on page 189.)

To order additional copies of
*With Liberty & Justice For All*
Send $8.95 each (postpaid)
to
Covenant House Books
P.O. Box 4690
Sevierville, TN 37864

Quantity Discounts

| | |
|---|---|
| 10-29 Copies | $5.56 each* |
| 30-99 Copies | $4.77 each* |
| 100+ Copies | $3.98 each* |

*Add 10% to order for postage
TN residents add 8% Sales Tax to order

# Aids
## THE UNNECESSARY EPIDEMIC
by
### Dr. Stanley K. Monteith

When the history of the AIDS epidemic is written — if anyone is left to write it! — it will be recorded that this was an unnecessary epidemic. It is a disease which is being treated like it was a civil rights issue instead of a deadly, contagious, communicable disease.

Dr. Monteith spent four years researching and writing this monumental book. He tells the story from the beginning — to the sad end — of this devastating disease. He tells what you MUST do in order to protect your family from this dreaded plague.

Dr. Monteith's solution begins with Christian morality right from the Bible and he calls for the use of time-proven health techniques by the health profession.

The AIDS epidemic can no longer be swept under the rug. What began as a homosexual disease is spreading into the heterosexual population and young people of both sexes are vulnerable to this awesome epidemic.

This book will give you valuable information and it will also shock you to discover that AIDS could have been stopped years ago, but is being allowed to spread across the land and infect millions.

This is the first time in the recorded history of mankind when society refused to protect itself from a deadly communicable disease.

What is the difference in the HIV virus and AIDS? Why is testing not being done to isolate and stop the spread? Why do politicians oppose testing? How can you really protect your family? Why won't condoms produce safe sex? Can deep kissing transmit the HIV virus? Is it safe for people with AIDS to work in the food industry? Can children with the HIV virus pass it on to other children in school? Are healthcare workers protected from the HIV virus? Is the virus carried by mosquitos? Learn the answers to these and other important questions.

This large volume now only $16.95 postpaid. Two copies postpaid for only $30. (Booksellers write for quantity discounts.)

**Covenant House Books**
**P. O. Box 4690, Sevierville, TN 37864**

# TO STAND ALONE
## Inside the KKK for the FBI

### by
### Delmar Daniel Dennis

The incredible story of violence and murder in Mississippi in the 1960s. An inside look at the Ku Klux Klan, The FBI, The John Birch Society, Civil Rights, J. Edgar Hoover, and Martin Luther King, Jr. A first person account by a Christian Reconstructionist.

Delmar Dennis was the American Party's nominee for President of the United States in 1984 and 1988. He is one of the most controversial characters of our time. Read his own story and make up your own mind about his position on the vital issues which face the American people today.

Shot at, spat upon, jailed, hated — and loved, Delmar now tells it all in this new book which includes secret Klan documents, Congressional reports, news stories, and incidents from his own personal diary.

208 pages, paperback, $16.95 from:

**Covenant House Books**
**P. O. Box 4690**
**Sevierville, TN 37864**